DOMESTIC CULTURE IN THE MIDDLE EAST

An exploration of the household interior

Jennifer Scarce

N·M·S

NATIONAL MUSEUMS OF SCOTLAND

Published by the National Museums of Scotland
Chambers Street, Edinburgh EH1 1JF
in association with Curzon Press,
St John's Studios, Church Road, Richmond,
Surrey TW9 2QA

ISBN 07007 0460 4

British Library Cataloguing in Publishing Data
A catalogue record for this book is available from the
British Library

Designed and produced by the Publishing Office of
the National Museums of Scotland

Printed by Clifford Press Ltd, Coventry, Great Britain

Acknowledgements
Illustrations: Cover, 4, 6, 9, 11, 17, 19, 21 left, 22, 27, 28, 31, 33, 34, 36, 40, 41, 47 right, 48, 52, 58, 59, 60, 61, 62, 64, 65, 67, 69, 70 left and right, 71, 72, 73 left and right, 74, 77, 79, 80, 83 left and right, 84, 85 left and right, 86 right, 87, 89, 90, 91, 92, 94 top and bottom, 95 right, 99, 100, 101, 103, 105, 106, 108, 109: NMS. 10, 12, 14 top, 15, 18, 51, 56, 96, 104: by courtesy of the Board of Trustees of the Victoria & Albert Museum. 13, 21 right, 42 top and bottom, 47 left, 53, 54 left and right, 55 top and bottom, 86 left, 95 left: Jennifer Scarce. 14 bottom, 23: Les Editions Nagel. 24, 44: The Trustees of the National Library of Scotland. 32: Birmingham Museums and Art Gallery. 35, 38: Edinburgh University Library. 37 top: Trustees of the British Library. 37 bottom: Charles E Tuttle Co Inc. 49: KEA Publishing Services Ltd. 57: Staatliche Museen zu Berlin. 81, 107: Trustees of the British Museum.

We are grateful to the National Museums of Scotland Charitable Trust and the NMS
Department of History and Applied Art for support for this publication.

Cover
*An elegant couple enjoying a musical performance. Scene painted on a papier
mâché pen box. Iran, 19th century*

Contents

Introduction

Domestic Culture in the Middle East invites the reader to enter and enjoy wealthy urban homes in Turkey, Egypt and Iran between the sixteenth and nineteenth centuries. This was a period of flourishing traditional culture and also of change. Decoration and furnishing of the home was increasingly influenced by ideas imported from Europe. This led to a lively fusion of styles, but the Middle Eastern household itself, the extended family and its dependents, remained essentially unchanged, with the traditional relationships, daily routines and domestic celebrations continuing.

Family life took place in a domestic environment of material comfort secluded behind discreet façades. The distinctive features of an affluent domestic interior were textiles which provided household furnishing and clothing, functioned as symbols of power and social status and played a vital economic role in industry and trade. Delight in brilliant colour and an imaginative treatment of surface and texture are striking aspects of Middle Eastern textiles. These distinctive features also influenced architectural decoration, manuscript illumination and the ornament of ceramics, metalwork, leather and wood.

This rich interior life is strikingly demonstrated by the Middle Eastern collections of the National Museums of Scotland. This valuable resource includes many objects illustrating the arts of ceramics and glass, metalwork, painting and lacquer, textiles, dress and jewellery, from the ninth to the twentieth century. The collections began modestly in 1858 with the acquisition of dress and jewellery from Egypt and developed rapidly during the Directorship of Major General Sir Robert Murdoch Smith KCMG (1885-1900) who came to the Museum after a career as Director of the Persian Telegraph Service (1865-1888) and as pioneer scholar of Iranian art. Through his expert knowledge and contacts the Museum acquired a fine collection of Iranian art, notably of the seventeenth to the nineteenth century. Since his day the geographical range of the collections has expanded to include Arabia, Egypt, North Africa, Syria, Turkey, Central Asia and India.

The objects are displayed in a permanent exhibition, 'Within the Middle East', in the Royal Museum of Scotland, Chambers Street, Edinburgh. They are presented through an imaginative interpretation of furnishing, clothing and ornament in a Middle Eastern household. These themes are further traced and explored in this book, which focuses on three major cities of the Middle East, looking at domestic and social patterns of life and the material culture that expressed them. Certain patterns are also traced through the closely related cultures of India, where the rituals of birth, growing up and adulthood are joyfully celebrated in painting.

Embroidered wool patchwork hanging. Iran, Resht, early 19th century

5

1
THE CITY

Cups filled with sherbet of every hue
Shone as rifts in a cloud where the sun gleams through.
There were goblets of purest crystal filled
With wine and sweet odours with art distilled.
The golden cloth blazed like the sunlight; a whole
Cluster of stars was each silver bowl.

These tantalizing verses are from one of the most famous and poignant epics of classical Iranian literature, *Yusuf amd Zulaikha*. Written by the poet Jami in 1483, this epic poem has a theme common to Jewish, Christian and Islamic moral and literary culture. The Hebrew slave Joseph and the wife of the Egyptian official Potiphar, whose story is first told in the *Old Testament* book of Genesis, reappear in the *Qur'an* as Yusuf and Zulaikha. The poets of the Middle East developed this *Qur'anic* version into a tragic love story which combined both earthly passion and spiritual redemption. The poet's sumptuous images locate the characters of Yusuf and Zulaikha in an environment of considerable material comfort. Even in a rather stilted Victorian English translation the lines quoted above evoke a social life where luxurious interior decoration, crystal and silver were as important as food and drink. They occur in the most frequently interpreted episode where Zulaikha introduces Yusuf at a party she has given to her women friends in an attempt to justify her obsession. Their reactions to his beauty are dramatic and varied. Some faint, while others cut their hands instead of the oranges provided for their refreshment.

Illustrations of this story are revealing documents of material culture, furnishings, clothes, accessories and ornaments. In the illustration [opposite] Yusuf and Zulaikha adorn a small tray dated exactly to 1697 AD (1109 H) worked in the delicate art of painted papier mâché favoured for accessories such as pen, mirror and comb cases, and jewel and trinket boxes in middle-class and upper-class Iranian households. The scene is a well-tended garden lined with cypress trees where

Painted papier mâché tray. Zulaikha presents Yusuf to her friends. Iran, Isfahan, dated 1697 AD (1109 H)

flowering plants cluster around an ornamental pool. Zulaikha is seated on a carpet under an open kiosk draped with a textile awning. She and her friends are elegantly dressed in layers of closely-fitting garments in fabrics patterned with stripes and small repeated flowers, which were the urban fashions of late seventeenth-century Iran. Hair trained in tendrils is covered with fur-trimmed hats, diadems and shawls.

The only male in this female party is Yusuf, standing on the left dressed as a fashionable young courtier whose beauty is emphasized by the halo which enfolds him. Fine ceramic vases and bowls, brass incense burners and spouted ewers are both decorative and functional. Oranges appear in the abundance of fruits offered to guests. The scene offers a detailed picture of late seventeenth-century Iranian court society where entertainment in gardens well-secluded from the outside world was a favourite leisure activity. Gardens also provided a sympathetic environment for both the composition and reading of the poetry which is so profoundly admired in Iranian culture. It is arguable that the choice of a poetic theme for a comparatively modest object indicates a widespread appreciation of literature.

The tray was made during the reign of Shah Sultan Hussein (1694-1722) in the city of Isfahan. This city had flourished as the capital of Iran since 1598 and as a major urban centre in the Middle East. Its eminence ended abruptly after the Afghan invasion of 1722 and although its shattered architectural splendours survived to be admired by European visitors, its role had passed by 1786 to Tehran, which is still Iran's capital. Other great cities of the Middle East, however, competed with those of Iran for political, economic and cultural status. Chief among these was Istanbul, transformed since its capture as Constantinople in 1453 by Sultan Mehmet II (1451-81) into the capital of the Ottoman Turkish Empire. Cairo became the largest city of the medieval Middle East and survived as the capital of an Ottoman province. Such cities share, together with the provincial cities of the Middle East, an urban culture which reflects historical, economic, social, religious and ethnic diversity. The artefacts of their domestic interiors are a manifestation of this diversity.

During the sixteenth to nineteenth centuries, the period surveyed in this study, the Middle East was relatively tranquil. Most of its cities came under the continuous administration of the Ottoman Turkish Empire (1299-1924), which at its most powerful reached from Central Europe through Turkey and Iraq to the Arabian Gulf, penetrating the Crimea and the coasts of the Eastern Mediterranean and North Africa *en route*. Iran, apart from an interval of civil and military chaos in the mid-eighteenth century, was under the rulers of the Safavid (1501-1722) and Qajar (1786-1924) dynasties at this time.

There are great geographical variations in the Middle East, from the mountains of central Turkey and Iran to the lush greenery of Iran's Caspian shore. The Mediterranean coastal strip from Turkey to the North African coast is agricultural land; much of the

Cairo, street and mosque near the citadel. Count Amadeo Preziosi, c1850

8

The Maidan-i Shah (Royal Square) at Isfahan. Eugene-Napoleon Flandin, 1841

Arabian peninsula is desert. Cities grew up where there was access to food, water, transport and communication. Once established, these cities developed a rich social and cultural environment.

Istanbul has been occupied since its foundation in the seventh century BC as the modest Greek trading colony of Byzantium. The site commands the traditional trade routes between Europe, North Africa, the Black Sea, India and China and is of incomparable strategic importance. It grew rich from the trade in silks, spices and precious stones, and fed its citizens from the food-supplies which poured in from the fertile hinterland of Southern Europe. Cairo is equally remarkable for its continuity of occupation which can be traced from the Pharaonic settlements of Memphis and Giza through successive Greek, Roman, medieval, Ottoman and contemporary developments. Like Istanbul, it is located strategically on a great waterway, the river Nile, through which it controls access to Upper Egypt and the Sudan: its food supplies are from the fertile regions of the Nile Delta.

Iran's urban settlement pattern is more diffuse than that of Turkey or Egypt as, apart from the enclosed area of the Caspian Sea in the north and the Gulf in the south, the country is arid and lacks a source of water for use as a means of transport. Consequently Iran's major cities were generally situated on overland routes. Isfahan has a record of occupation since the late seventh century. It is located in a wide and fertile valley on the

Zayandehrud River. In this it is fortunate, as the supply of water has always been a problem in Iran, and here depended mainly on access to underground sources tapped through an ingenious system of irrigation channels. Water and food were equally important considerations in the transfer of the capital to the northern city of Tehran in 1786, which long enjoyed a reputation for the quality of its fruit and vegetable gardens and had access to water from the springs and channels of Mount Demavend.

Perhaps the most dynamic resource of the great cities was their populations, formed of both long-established and immigrant communities. A cosmopolitan society evolved. The advance of Islam as the dominant religion of the Middle East from the seventh century onwards imposed a shared cultural identity to which significant Jewish and Christian cultures contributed professional and commercial skills. Arabic, the liturgical language of Islam, functioned as a *lingua franca* also among communities whose native tongues were of Persian, Turkish, Armenian, Slav and Berber origin.

One of the continuing problems of cities concerned the accommodation of their inhabitants. Public requirements demanded administrative and religious buildings, communication networks, commercial areas, water and bathing facilities, while there was a need for private housing at all levels. Although the cities were notable for their

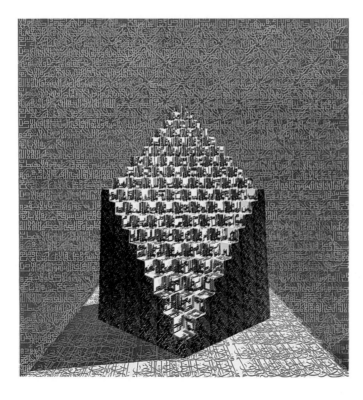

Screen-printed poster. Religious inscriptions in three styles of Arabic calligraphy. Egypt, Ahmed Moustafa, 1987

Istanbul, entrance to the Golden Horn. Count Amadeo Preziosi, 1853

cosmopolitan populations, Islamic law influenced attitudes towards private property. Islam emphasizes an individual's position both within the community of Muslim believers and within the family as the basic unit of social life. The *Qur'an* gives precise instructions on family relationships and obligations, and property and inheritance rights. By implication, especially in an urban context, every family has a right to live enclosed within its own house. This leads to a clear separation between public and private space. Public life takes place in the streets, the service and commercial sectors, while private life looks inwards to courtyards and rooms within walls. The two areas are articulated but not necessarily integrated.

This division in the functions of space varies depending on the topographical and historical circumstances of individual cities. Streets and buildings had to follow the contours of the land available. Very rarely was it possible to plan and construct anew. The Ottoman Turks inherited the remains of Byzantine Constantinople which were in a ruinous state. There were desolate open spaces, neglected houses and gardens, and the walled jumble of randomly assembled pavilions, reception halls, chapels and private apartments of the former imperial palace at the south-east end of the city. Muslim dynasties which followed the Arab conquest of Egypt had to manage the ever-increasing layers of their predecessors' building programmes. In Iran, conversion of the provincial town of Tehran into a capital city required constant repairs and extensions to existing structures as well as new building projects. Eventually, ambitious programmes of the 1850s-70s, which introduced European-influenced elements of planning and architecture, resulted in a blend of conservatism and innovation in building in all three capitals. Many of the old maze-like traditional quarters were swept away while others survived to be renovated in appearance rather than function.

Yet it is possible to identify the development of the main zones which serviced the basic needs of the city. The structures built for defence and protection formed a distinctive physical boundary. Traditionally, fortified citadels and massive walls were built which either sealed off sections of the city or encircled it. Istanbul's strategic position was strengthened by the series of walls of late Roman and Byzantine origin which linked the Golden Horn and the Sea of Marmora to protect the city on the landward side. Another chain of walls extended round the extreme south-eastern point containing the first of the city's seven hills, the site of the old Byzantine imperial palace and the complex of Topkapi Saray, the Ottoman seat of government, court and royal household. Various attempts were made to provide Cairo with an effective defence system. The most spectacular and effective was the scheme which Sultan Salah-al-Din (Saladin) planned and completed between 1171 and 1182. It included the two main settlements of the city within a walled enclosure commanded by the citadel on the high ground between the Nile and the Muqattam Hills. Successive plans of Tehran show how the city developed radially from an irregular polygonal shape within a retaining moat and wall complete with watchtowers and six gates constructed during the sixteenth century. By the reign of Fath Ali Shah Qajar (1797-1834) these structures had been repaired many times and the gatehouses were embellished with glittering tilework depicting the exploits of the Iranian

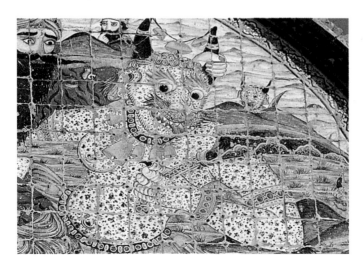

Iran, Semnan. City gate of 1884 AD (1302 H) decorated with a tilework panel showing Rustam fighting the White Div.

hero Rustam locked in combat with the White Div, a speckled grotesque creature.

Closely linked to defence systems were complexes devoted to the household of the ruler, his family and entourage, and the offices of the state administration. These were comparable to small cities. Such a mingling of private and public functions resulted in an often haphazard architectural programme as buildings were added and adapted. Often complexes were built on existing foundations, as it was reasonable to continue using an ideal site. The most splendid example of this is the Topkapi Saray in Istanbul built on Byzantine foundations south of the great cathedral of Saint Sophia. According to the Greek chronicler Kritovoulos, Sultan Mehmet II gave orders in 1459 for the erection of a palace on the point of old Byzantium which stretches out into the sea – a palace that should outshine all and be more marvellous than preceding palaces in looks, size, cost and gracefulness. The Sultan's creation eventually covered an enormous area within a high wall, planned as a series of four linked courts, two devoted to public and administrative functions and two to private audiences and domestic life, concealed by fortified gates and entrances, to which access was progressively limited. His successors added to this structure. Eventually the four courts supported a rambling assortment of administrative buildings, kitchen and stable quarters, schools, libraries, mosques, pavilions and private apartments set in agreeable gardens.

Again, in Tehran also the administrative centre and the royal residence were enclosed within a single walled area popularly known as the Arg. Here, however, development was more random and diffuse than in Istanbul. The Arg shared its northern wall with that of the city's ramparts while the buildings within,

Portrait of Fath Ali Shah (1797-1834) in oils on canvas. Abdullah Khan, early 19th century

Opposite
Top: *Istanbul, view of the courts of the Topkapi Saray. Gaspard Fossati, 1852*

Bottom: *Tehran, buildings of the Gulestan Palace inside the walls of the Arg. Mahmoud Saba, 1864*

which formed the Gulestan Palace, consisted mainly of independent units such as open-sided audience chambers, courtyards and pavilions among luxuriant gardens watered by ornamental pools and channels. These amenities were the work of Fath Ali Shah who saw the palace as both a suitable framework for his own magnificence and an inviting refuge from the heat and dust of the outside world. Cairo's citadel more resembled a military stronghold. Within its extensive enclosure were housed a defence tower and the barracks of the royal guard as well as the palaces of the Sultan, his household and officials.

Between and around most city walls and royal complexes were the quarters where the needs of a city's everyday life were served. Although their streets gave a superficially crowded and chaotic impression they did, in fact, operate to a logical modular plan. Networks of main streets both provided routes for communication and divided the city into service and residential quarters. Streets within each quarter were often cramped and narrow, dirty and muddy in winter and dusty in summer. The basic requirements were housing for residents, which varied according to their status and wealth, a local mosque, synagogue or church in Jewish and Christian sections, shops and market and a public bath.

Definition was given to a city by the great religious and commercial complexes. These were built at strategic locations near the ruler's palace, at the intersections of main roads and on high points such as the seven hills of Istanbul. The patrons of these public works were the rulers, their families and wealthy private citizens. Provision, construction and maintenance were financed through the Islamic form of charitable bequest known as *waqf*: that is, revenue-generating property - rentable land, houses or shops - donated or bequeathed in perpetuity for the support of pious works which could range in scope from a mosque to a local drinking fountain. This aspect of Islam which combined religious and commercial enterprise was expressed in the proximity of mosque and bazaar. Istanbul and Tehran are particularly distinctive examples of the interdependence of such buildings.

Istanbul's topography, dominated by the domes and minarets of the great imperial mosque complexes, illustrates *waqf* bequests on a grand scale. The mosques of Sultan Mehmet II (1451-81), Sultan Selim I 1512-20), Sultan Süleyman the Magnificent (1520-66) and his daughter Mihrimah command the fourth, fifth, third and sixth hills respectively. Such mosques were complemented by equally impressive buildings dedicated to religious, educational and charitable functions. Equal importance was given to the needs of commerce. Istanbul was notable for the range of services which it could offer to both residents and travellers. The main business district, located in the heart of the old city, consisted of a network of intersecting streets flanked by open markets. *Hans* or caravanserais offered accommodation for travelling merchants, storage for their goods, offices for the transaction of business and workshop space. The enclosed *bedesten* specialized in the sale of luxuries and the shops of the *çarşı* sold an enormous range of house-

Women shopping in the silk market of Istanbul. Count Amadeo Preziosi, 1853

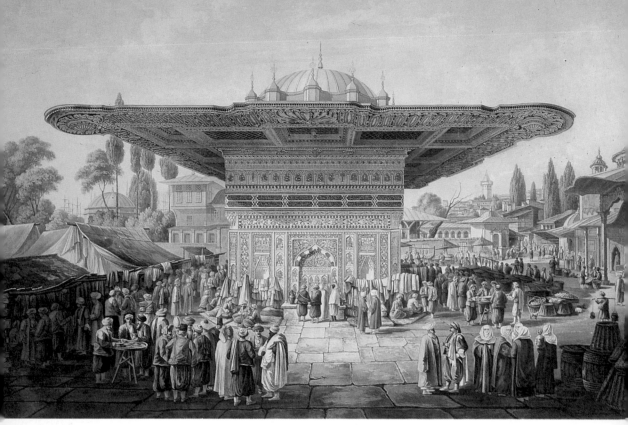

Istanbul, the fountain at Tophane. William Page, 1829

hold goods. Outside the covered areas the open markets or bazaars dealt mainly in food. The close relationship between religious and commercial functions was emphasized as income from each *han* and *bedesten* contributed to the maintenance of mosques.

Other important features of Istanbul's infrastructure concerned water, transport and manufacture. The Ottoman Turks upgraded and extended the old Byzantine water system soon after their conquest of 1453. Water from the Belgrad Forest came to the city via a system of dams, reservoirs and aqueducts to be stored in water towers and enormous underground cisterns for distribution throughout the city. Although water was free, only the Topkapi Saray, important buildings and wealthy households had their own supplies, so donations of the beautiful public fountains around the city were noteworthy acts of charity. The main streets, which were paved, were used to transport goods and people but water transport was more effective. Merchant ships and passenger ferries regularly sailed along the shores of the Golden Horn and the Bosphorus. While Istanbul's unrivalled geographical and political position commanded all essential resources, the city was also a manufacturing centre in its own right. Specialist ateliers produced goods exclusively for the Topkapi Saray and other imperial establishments;

state factories made arms and uniforms for the army and navy; clusters of workshops made wares for sale in the covered markets. The outlying suburbs furnished space for the less salubrious trades, such as the tanning and working of leather which dominated the quarter of Yedikule near the old Byzantine walls.

The integration of homes into this impressive infrastructure reflected social status. Broadly speaking social stratification was vertical, with the rich living on the upper slopes of the city and the poor crowded in shabby wooden houses below. The shores of the upper Bosphorus were also lined with spacious wealthy homes within gardens. Individual character was often given to a residential quarter through the presence of some outstanding feature. The quarter of Eyüp at the head of the Golden Horn is centred around the tomb of Eyüp Ensari, the standard bearer of the Prophet Muhammad who died during the first Arab siege of Constantinople in 674. Eyüp developed as a centre of pilgrimage, as a burial place for pious Muslims and as a wealthy residential area. Istanbul's non-Muslim communities lived in segregated quarters. The most colourful and lively was Pera across the Golden Horn, where local Greeks lived together with the European diplomatic and commercial missions.

Tehran is more compact, located at the base of the foothills of the Elburz mountains dominated by the peak of Mount Demavend, which gives the city a vertical alignment both physically and socially. The administrative quarters of the Arg and neighbouring religious and commercial institutions were in the south of the city while the summer residences of the Shahs and their court occupied the north, extending beyond the city wall into the surrounding hills.

Document wallet of green silk velvet on leather embroidered in silver. The owner's name JACOBUS BISANTIUS DE HOCHPIED, probably a Dutch merchant, is concealed under the flap, dated 1697.

Unlike the Ottoman Sultans who resided permanently in Topkapi Saray, the Qajar Shahs migrated annually between the winter residence of the Gulestan Palace within the Arg and several summer establishments which varied from seasonal hunting lodges to formally planned buildings. Although the distances travelled were small by modern standards the migrations were cumbersome journeys involving the transportation of the Shah's household and officials with all their luggage in an assortment of carriages and carts. The Qajars continued to migrate even after Tehran was rebuilt in the 1860s, maintaining a sentimental link with their nomadic tribal past and a practical desire to escape to the comforts of the cool northern hills in the heat of summer.

Tehran's main religious building, located close to the south wall of the Arg, was the large mosque built in the time of Fath Ali Shah between 1808 and 1813. Extensions into neighbouring buildings through common walls and passages created a close relationship with the bazaar booths clustered around the mosque. Both Fath Ali Shah and Nasiruddin Shah (1848-96) extended the bazaar area, roofed its streets and alleys and constructed new shops and caravanserais. They also made efforts to improve the water supply which depended on an intricate system of water channels which were filled from wells and underground sources in the mountains north of the city. Adjacent to the bazaar were the small workshops of metalsmiths and potters, while spreading further south and outwith the limits of the city walls were extensive brick kilns which supplied the city's main building material. Networks of streets radiated out from the complex of Arg, mosque and bazaar dividing the city into residential units intersected by narrow alleys. As in Istanbul the poorer inhabitants lived in crowded conditions while the wealthier citizens' homes were situated to the north and east.

Cities are never static. All three capitals had to cope with a constant stream of immigrants who would either join communities already established in the city or camp in squatter settlements on the outskirts. This brought severe pressures on services and housing. Buildings were frequently at risk of fire and flood; they fell into decay or simply were no longer suited to their original purpose. There was continual building and rebuilding. Until the nineteenth century this constant change had proceeded at a measured pace, gradually modifying the shape of cities but retaining their traditional orientation. During the 1850s-70s, however, ambitious construction programmes in all three capitals broke this traditional pattern through clearance of old quarters and relocation of each city's working centre. Various factors contributed towards these programmes of modernization. By the late eighteenth century the Ottoman Sultans were actively seeking contacts with Europe and were recruiting technical, architectural and military expertise to develop and re-define the traditional institutions of the Empire.

The functions of the Topkapi Saray had gradually diminished as the administration moved out to ministries in the city. The royal residence was abandoned as it was considered old-fashioned and inconvenient. Parts had already been destroyed in fires which had regularly swept through the city from the sixteenth century onwards. Sultan Mahmut II (1808-39) moved, in 1826, to a new palace at Beşiktaş, on the Pera side of

Photograph of Nasiruddin Shah (1848-96) taken in 1873.

Istanbul, entrance gate of the Dolmabahce Palace.

the Golden Horn, thus shifting the focus of the city to the north. These changes coincided with his destruction of the Janissery corps and the dissolution of their headquarters. He replaced them with regiments trained along modern lines and housed them in barracks located outside the land walls of the city, at Pera and at Haydarpaşa on the Asian side of the Bosphorus. His successors continued his policy of isolating the old city and separating the administration from the imperial household by building more palaces, such as the splendid Dolmabahçe Palace, commissioned by Sultan Abdul Medjit I (1839-61), completed in 1853, whose Italianate façade and terrace now dominate the shore at Beşiktaş. All these moves affected the residential pattern of the city. Wealthy citizens had always maintained summer houses (*yalıs*) on the shores of the Bosphorus. By the late 1850s they had moved permanently to these homes, following the Ottoman court northwards.

While these changes in Istanbul were inevitable they were encouraged through direct Ottoman contacts with Paris which had been transformed during the 1850s-60s into a city of grand boulevards linked by gardens and squares, under the direction of Baron Haussmann. The Universal Exhibition held in 1867 enabled delegations from Turkey, Egypt and Iran to display both their industrial products and handicrafts, and to see Haussmann's achievements for themselves. The Ottoman Sultan Abdul Aziz (1861-76) the Khedive Ismail (1863-79) of Egypt and some Iranian officials visited the Exhibition and were guided around Paris. These experiences hastened plans for municipal improvement in their homelands. In Istanbul the Pera quarter was subject to the

Photograph of the Khedive Ismail taken in about 1870.

most ambitious experiments in town planning and administration. By the late 1860s the old walls surrounding the quarter were pulled down and the Galata Bridge was built to link Pera to the old city. Broad streets and squares were constructed and lined with smart shops and apartments. In Cairo, the Khedive Ismail, who had already considered ideas for modernizing parts of the city, completely changed them after his visit to Paris. He decided to build the spacious extensions of Ismailiyeh and Ezbekiyeh to the north and west of the old town and to move the business and administrative sectors there.

It was Tehran which perhaps saw the most extreme and rapid transformation. The city, still confined within the much repaired sixteenth-century walls, was no longer able to function effectively. The population had increased to such an extent that settlement had sprawled beyond the city walls creating problems of security. A network of roads was needed to improve communication and transport, and the water supply system needed to be upgraded as the city was often flooded. Nasiruddin Shah's decision to reconstruct Tehran was taken in December 1867, a few months after the Paris Exhibition. He began by demolishing the old walls and by bringing the northern suburbs within the city to enlarge it to four times its original size. He enclosed this area within a new set of octagonal walls complete with towers, a moat and twelve tile-decorated gates. In these architectural details he favoured tradition.

The immediate result of this expansion was to locate the administrative and business quarters firmly in the south of the city. The Arg continued to function as both winter residence and administrative centre, but the Gulestan Palace was transformed by Nasiruddin Shah

Tehran, Lalezar Avenue. Mahmoud Saba, 1871

through demolition of his predecessors' buildings and construction of new reception and domestic units during the years 1867-92. He maintained the Qajar tradition of migrating to summer residences and commissioned several palaces in the northern hills. The square to the south of the Arg which gave access to the bazaar area was enlarged and improved. The most significant result of Nasiruddin Shah's building programme was the development of north Tehran into spacious and fashionable suburbs. A network of broad streets leading from a magnificent new square linked the city to routes to the settlements outside the walls. Between these streets residential accommodation evolved dominated by the elegant houses and gardens of the rich.

2
THE HOUSE

> It is situated on one of the most delightful parts of the canal [the Bosphorus] with a fine wood on the side of a hill behind it. The extent of it is prodigious; the guardian assured me there is 800 rooms in it. I will not answer for that number since I did not count them but 'tis certain the number is very large and the whole adorned with a profusion of marble, gilding and the most exquisite painting of fruit and flowers.

A letter from Lady Mary Wortley Montagu gives an enthusiastic description of her visit in 1718 to the palace of Fatma, the fourteen-year-old daughter of Sultan Ahmet III (1703-30). Her letter indicates Fatma's importance to her father and family at least in terms of the extravagance of the residence built for her. This passage also shows how much a fine view was cherished and considered necessary in the choice of a location.

Characteristic of Turkish domestic architecture was the imaginative treatment of space and the creation of gardens which indicated a close relationship between internal and external environments. In Istanbul itself homes were enclosed within gardens, while the shores of the Bosphorus provided panoramic views. These features were the preserve of the upper and middle classes. Homes in the poorest quarters of the city managed to find a space for a few plants in pots or window-boxes. Those with homes in provincial cities such as Bursa, Safranbolu and Amasya also valued gardens and locations of natural beauty.

An equally keen understanding of the balance between buildings and enclosed space is seen in the domestic architecture of Iran. The enlargement of Tehran during the building programmes of the 1860s formally acknowledges this. Spacious homes in gardens were brought within reach of the services and security of the city walls. Variations of this classic home scheme were also built in Iran's provinces, for example, in and around the cities of Isfahan, Shiraz and Kerman. Cairo's city area was more congested, yet building solutions were found which allowed for the insertion of garden plots and arbours within the house plan.

Istanbul, houses on the Bosphorus. Frank Bartlett, 1835

The provision of public open space was particularly appreciated by those who could not afford their own gardens. There were the courtyards and gardens of the mosques and shrines. Large graveyards with flowers and trees between the tombstones surrounded Istanbul, great cemeteries spread out below the citadel of Cairo full of the imposing tombs of rulers and their families, while the foothills to the north of Tehran were populated by villages.

Although homes in Middle Eastern cities had their own local character in terms of design and decoration, general principles of definition and separation of public and private space were followed, which survived the modernization programmes of the mid-nineteenth century. An elegant palace, for example, decorated with columns and pediments inspired by classical European models would be as much screened from public view behind high walls as a traditional house. In the compact streets of a city's residential quarters, deceptively modest entrances concealed the richness of the interior. In the suburbs locked gates set in plain retaining walls discouraged unwanted attention.

The importance of interior space is reflected in Middle Eastern painting. Manuscripts of the historical chronicles and epic poems are sumptuously illustrated with narrative scenes which concentrate on the interior. Yusuf and Zulaikha, for example, are confined in their garden. Outdoor scenes, though exquisitely drawn and painted, give no suggestion of the panorama of landscape as understood in European art.

The houses of Istanbul are distinguished by the flexibility with which their building units were planned and constructed. A standard was established by Sultan Mehmet II, whose work at Topkapi Saray was much praised by the Greek historian Kritovoulos. Writing on its completion by 1465 he says:

> Also he finished the palace, the most beautiful of all the buildings, equally for the view, for usefulness, for pleasure, for ornamentation; it left nothing to be desired, even by comparison with the most ancient and most marvellous edifices of the world ...

The private apartments of Topkapi Saray were grouped around the third and fourth courts. Domestic life at all levels required a clear division between the *selamlık*, the men's quarters where visitors were received, and the *haremlik*, the private quarters where only members of the family, the women and their female friends spent their time. In the palace this meant rigorously enforced seclusion of the women, which is clearly illustrated in the plan and location of rooms. Within the third court, the buildings combine a series of intersecting rooms around the courtyard walls with independent units, such as a throne room, a library and a mosque. The throne room, reached through a handsomely decorated gate under a deep porch, functioned as a *selamlık* with strictly limited access. It was a small pavilion of two rooms under a heavy roof with overhanging eaves supported on columns, creating a covered walkway around all four sides. Here the Ottoman Sultan would receive his most senior officials and foreign ambassadors.

Istanbul, woman and child visiting a cemetery. Count Amadeo Preziosi, 1853

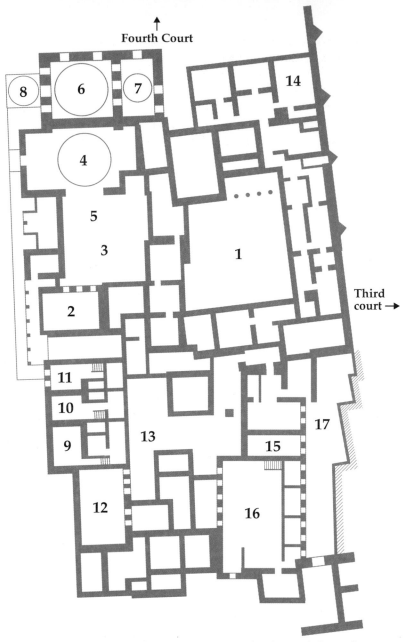

Istsanbul, plan of the haremlik *of the Topkapi Saray. Drawn by Tim Smith from a plan in* Architecture, Ceremonial, and Power, *by Gülru Necipoğlu*

1 Sultan's mother's court
2 Sultan's mother's reception room
3 Sultan's mother's bath
4 Sultan's reception hall
5 Sultan's bath
6 Sultan Murat III's (1574-95) pavilion
7 Vestibule of Sultan Murat III's pavilion
8 Sultan Ahmet I's (1603-17) pavilion
9 Suite of the first wife
10 Suite of the second wife
11 Suite of the third wife
12 and 13 Bedrooms and court of the palace women
14 Suite of the princes
15 School of the princes
16 and 17 Bedrooms and court of the black eunuchs

28

The *haremlik* is located on the left side of the palace well behind the third and fourth courts, reached through a discreet entrance tucked away in a corner of the second court. It is a self-sufficient unit, separate from the basic palace plan of four longitudinally connected courts. It is an intricate labyrinth which had steadily increased from the sixteenth to eighteenth century to about 300 surprisingly small units - rooms, courtyards, intimate gardens, stairs and passages.

This apparent confusion of space is actually a logically connected series of residential modules, providing the apartments of the Sultan, his mother (arguably the most powerful member of the Ottoman household), the palace women, young princes and princesses. Each apartment was formed of rooms of one or two storeys around a square or rectangular vestibule or open court. The apartment of the Sultan's mother is probably the most logically planned and spacious example consisting of a suite of reception and private rooms, with bath and prayer room around a large square court.

Despite this careful balance between rooms and space, the overwhelming impression in the *haremlik* is claustrophobic. The informal arrangement of buildings in the fourth and last court of the palace, however, gave opportunities for a more relaxed environment. It consists of a landscaped garden on several levels, descending from a marble terrace and pool, with a splendid view of the Golden Horn. The buildings within the garden, mainly of seventeenth- and eighteenth-century date, are an attractive combination of open-sided octagonal kiosks with deep porches, and pavilions with low ceilings and large windows. Although these buildings were primarily for the use of the Sultan, there was a long corridor from the *haremlik* to the marble terrace where women could be invited to join him. So deeply ingrained was this method of household planning that the Europeanized nineteenth-century palaces which replaced Tokpapi Saray show how their structures were modified to accommodate it. At Dolmabahçe for example, completed in 1853, the enormous ornamented reception hall is surrounded by rooms divided into *selamlık* and *haremlik* quarters which look inwards. On a more restrained scale, these palace forms were re-interpreted in the homes of Istanbul's wealthy citizens.

The most affluent and important members of Ottoman Turkish society, such as the great officials of the state, and members of the legal and religious establishment, had a choice of residence. The *konak* was a town house and the *yalı* was built on the shores of the Bosphorus to which the household could retreat for the summer. By the late nineteenth century the *yalı* in many cases had become the main residence and was continuously occupied throughout the year. The *konak* could be set within a garden behind a high wall, but many directly overlooked the street. Whatever style was chosen, they were both protected by locked entrances. The most immediate feature of the exterior of a *konak* was the picturesque overlapping of the storeys. The two or three storeys each projected well over the one below, supported on curved beams to give the effect of a closed balcony. The reasons for this structural feature were practical as well as aesthetic. It increased the area of the upper part of the *konak* and protected the entrance and lower walls from sun and rain. Each storey had a row of windows securely shuttered and screened with wooden lattices and metal gratings inhibiting prying eyes and light. The structure was then covered with a gently sloping roof with extremely wide eaves projecting up to two metres beyond the upper storey.

Behind the façade a city *konak* could have up to 30 or 40 rooms. Within the main entrance the home divided more-or-less symmetrically into the *selamlık* and *haremlik*, which usually took the form of two open courts linked by a narrow corridor. Covered variations of this plan had the *selamlık* on the first floor above service quarters and the *haremlik* tucked away on the top floor. Within each courtyard, arrangement and function of space was similar. Around the *selamlık* at ground level were stables and storage rooms for household supplies and quarters for menservants. On the next floor was the main public area of the *selamlık*, the *divankhana*, where visitors were received and business was transacted. This room was usually divided into two sections, a lower section near the door and a raised alcove lined with cushions around the walls where the male members of the family received their guests.

The courtyard of the *haremlik* was more intimate as it was private. Storerooms at ground level enclosed a garden. An entrance led into a vestibule lined with more storage rooms and sleeping quarters for domestic servants. Stairs led up to the reception room which divided as in the *selamlık* and was used for female guests and close relations. In both sections rooms surrounding the reception room were flexible and could function as additional sitting or sleeping areas.

Location of the service quarters varied according to the size and area of the *konak*. Kitchens were separate buildings in a courtyard or large garden, which contained brick ovens and large shallow troughs of charcoal. There was also a small kitchen within the *haremlik*, for the preparation of coffee, tea, and delicacies such as rose-petal and melon jams, and compotes of quince and pumpkin, which were offered to guests. Some of the rooms contained jugs and water taps for washing, while the grandest households had their own *hammam* – bath house – with hot and cold rooms.

The *yalı* on the shores of the Bosphorus was an informal and graceful interpretation of the *konak* within a garden. Entrance was gained through a gate in the high retaining wall on the land side which opened into gardens. The *yalı* itself was an extended building of one or two storeys with wide, lightly-framed windows overlooking the waters of the Bosphorus. Viewed from the opposite shore the façade, with a deeply projecting upper storey supported on curved beams, created the same picturesque effect as that of the city *konak*. Within the *yalı* a large hall with high ceilings separated the traditional *selamlık* and *haremlik* with their own suites of reception and supporting rooms. Here was more scope for variation. Sometimes the *selamlık* and *haremlik* were separate buildings, sometimes they were on different floors, sometimes the *haremlik* dominated the plan. Kiosks and pavilions, often of eccentric form and decoration, in the gardens contributed to an atmosphere of relaxed informality.

Gardens were more than just an agreeable background environment. They were admired and cultivated for their own sake by Sultans, their families and court. One of the most energetic and resourceful gardeners was Sultan Mehmet II. He planned the original gardens of the Topkapi Saray and enjoyed digging and planting them. There were also gardens open to the Istanbul public. Turkish gardeners had access to many exotic plants, bulbs and seeds, which were sent to Istanbul either as gifts to the Sultan's household, or for sale in the city's markets. Plans were imaginative and varied as the Turks preferred pleasing irregularity where flower beds, fountains, pools and parlours mingled, to the formal symmetry of Iranian gardens.

Although houses of the wealthy in Cairo resembled the Istanbul *konak* in their general plan, when new suburbs were developed in the late nineteenth century, some were built with lofty roofs equipped with wide windows in a style which mixed Turkish *yalı* and European architectural features. While fashionable, such houses did not suit the climate, as they were too hot in summer. The traditional house plan was practical and provided seclusion and protection from the heat of summer.

The house's discreet façade masked the life of the interior. One or two upper storeys, where windows were screened with carved wooden lattices, projected onto curved supporting arches over the blank wall of the ground floor. As in Istanbul, this feature maximized space, and regulated light and heat from the street. There were many variations to the main principles of planning which gave much idiosyncratic charm to the interior. The entrance led into a sharply angled passageway which opened into the courtyard of the men's quarters or *selamlık*. This contained, besides the stables and storage rooms, the main kitchen of the household and an open kiosk which was used as a reception area during the summer. Otherwise a formal room (*mandara*) was used

Cairo, private houses of the 1830s.

Cairo, courtyard of the painter's house. John Frederick Lewis, c1851

for the reception of male guests. A door at the furthermost corner of the courtyard led into the *harem* which consisted of suites of living rooms, grouped around the main family room which usually had a high-domed ceiling lit with panes of coloured glass. It was often divided into raised alcoves. Stairs led up to more rooms, terraces, balconies and a summer sitting room which was open along one side for the sake of coolness. As in Istanbul, households of the wealthy had their own bathhouses. Depending on the resources of the family it was possible to multiply storeys and units.

In Tehran and other major cities of Iran, the palaces and houses of the wealthy which have survived are mainly nineteenth century. They show a very different interpretation of the basic principles of residential architecture. Buildings were still enclosed within high retaining walls, and the segregation of the men's quarters (*biruni*) from the women's quarters (*andarun*) was strictly observed. A Tehran town house or country retreat

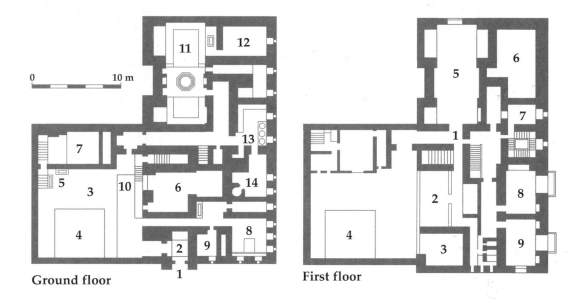

Ground floor

0   10 m

First floor

Cairo, plan of a wealthy house. Drawn by Tim Smith from a plan in The Beauty of Cairo *by GSP Freeman-Grenville.*

Ground floor

1 Entrance	7 Servants' quarters
2-9 Men's quarters	8-9 Stables
2 Vestibule	10 Entrance to women's
3 Courtyard	quarters
4 Reception kiosk	11 Family living area
5 Fountain	12 Sleeping area
6 Reception room	13 Kitchen
	14 Bakery

First floor

1 Entrance to women's quarters
2 Summer room
3 Sleeping area
4 Guest room
5-6 Living rooms
7-9 Women's rooms

presented a blank wall to the outside world interrupted only by a discreet entrance or high gate. Within an enclosure, the garden or courtyard functioned as a generously proportioned extension of the building units with a close spatial relationship between them. The palaces of the Qajar Shahs, their extended families and senior officials were spacious enough to accommodate independent buildings within a landscaped garden. Graceful octagonal pavilions, rectangular buildings enclosing open courtyards, deep-columned porches (*talars*) open on one or three sides, were grouped in an informal modular plan. The buildings were flexible and varied in function. The porch, for example, could be an entrance, an audience hall (*divankhana*) a sleeping area in hot weather, or a balcony if raised on a second or third storey. Juxtaposition of levels added interest to a building. Several storeys of low-ceilinged rooms were grouped around a deep porch all interlinked by a network of passages.

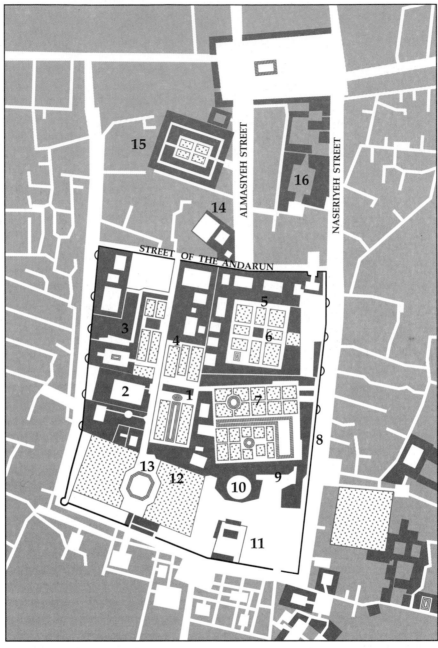

Tehran, the Gulestan Palace. From a plan drawn by Dr Feuvrier, Nasiruddin Shah's French doctor between 1889 and 1892. Tim Smith

1 Throne room
2 Royal stables
3 Palace guards' quarters
4 War office and palace of Naib es-Saltaneh, 3rd son of Nasiruddin Shah

5 Royal andarun
6 Nasiruddin Shah's private appartment
7 Palace gardens
8 Private residence
9 Wind tower

10 Theatre built by Nasiruddin Shah
11 Dr Feuvrier's house
12 Registry
13 Plaza of the Arg
14 Mosque

15 Arsenal
16 Dar Al-Funun – Tehran polytechnic

Tehran, Fath Ali Shah's reception porch in the Gulestan Palace. Eugène-Napoleon Flandin, 1839-41

This aesthetic is seen in both the Gulestan Palace within the Arg of Tehran and in the summer palaces north of the city. Fath Ali Shah (1797-1834) had built an imposing *talar* porch which he used for formal audiences and the reception of guests, and separate pavilions and women's quarters. His successor Nasiruddin Shah (1848-96), although influenced by contemporary European architectural style, continued the tradition of separate buildings during his renovation of the palace between 1867 and 1892. He kept Fath Ali Shah's *talar*, but constructed a mansion with a grand stair leading up to a huge audience hall and other reception rooms, a suite of private apartments for himself, and an *andarun* court.

The Gulestan Palace is distinguished for its gardens, laid out in a formal scheme of water channels intersecting at ornamental pools, flower beds and trees. While gardens were much admired throughout the Middle East, they have long played a central role in domestic architecture in Iran. Archaeological surveys have revealed plans of extensive gardens, ante-dating the arrival of Islam in the mid-seventh century, which show the origins of the classic geometric scheme. These Iranian gardens were an earthly paradise providing a refuge from the heat of the summer. It is believed that such gardens inspired the many descriptions of Paradise in the *Qur'an*.

Iran, Fath Ali Shah's summer palace of Qasr-i Qajar. Pascal Coste, 1839-41

Variety in the garden was achieved through the choice of flowers - roses, peonies or irises for example - and of trees such as cypress, orange or pomegranate. Terraces and channels could be added, and fish and ducks introduced. The summer palace Qasr-i Qajar built by Fath Ali Shah in 1807 dramatically illustrates the importance of gardens. The palace apartments are reached through a series of ascending garden terraces linked by cascading waterfalls. The summer palace of Nasiruddin Shah, Ishratabad, built in

Iran, the andarun *of Nasiruddin Shah's summer palace of Ishratabad, 1888.*

Opposite
Knotted wool carpet with a formal garden scheme. A contemporary Romanian interpretation of a traditional Iranian design, 1981.

Iran, the house and garden of Hussein Khan at Tabriz. Eugene-Napoleon Flandin, 1839-41

1888 near Qasr-i Qajar, shows a personal and imaginative interpretation of buildings within a garden. Here the *andarun* was built as seventeen independent chalets around a great oval lake.

All of these buildings are on a grand scale. Yet equally spacious and harmonious effects were created where the garden area was confined to a smaller domestic courtyard. Usually the courts of the *biruni* and *andarun* were linked by a discreet connecting passage, but they could also be completely separate enclosures within a large garden. In each quarter the rooms opened directly onto the court, which was usually planted with four beds of flowers and shrubs around a circular pool. The resulting house plan was versatile, functioning equally well in winter and summer. Deep columned porches were reception areas. In some homes they were fitted with sashed windows extending from ceiling to floor. Behind each porch were suites of sleeping and storage rooms. In a grand household, opposite sides of the court functioned as winter and summer quarters. An entrance led to a basement living room on the winter side, while staircases led up to a roof terrace on the summer side which functioned as an open-air sleeping area. Homes in the hottest central and southern regions of Iran followed the basic plan but were distinguished by tall square towers whose ribbed exteriors led to ventilation shafts which drew air down to the rooms below.

The materials and methods available for construction and decoration led to regional variations which contributed to the individual character of a household. A first impression of Istanbul might suggest that the principal building material was stone: the grey limestone for the great mosques and the silver-veined white marble reserved for facing, panels and openwork balconies seem to predominate. This is quite misleading. Expensive materials were found only in major public buildings. Domestic architecture at all levels of society was of wood, which explains why so many homes were destroyed during fires which regularly devastated Istanbul. Even the Topkapi Saray's buildings were originally of wood, enclosed within a stone retaining wall, and only gradually replaced by more substantial structures.

There were excellent reasons for the widespread use of wood. It was plentiful and cheap, with supplies brought in from Anatolia and the forests of the eastern European provinces to replenish local sources. It was practical and light compared to stone, important factors in a city which is located in an earthquake zone. In Istanbul's damp and humid climate wood dealt with water better than stone. Wooden homes could be quick to construct and allowed experiment and exploration in decorative detail. In a town *konak* the foundations and ground floor were built of stone, from which the storeys of

Iran, from a plan of the andarun *of a wealthy Iranian household of the late 19th century drawn by Jeanne Dieulafoy,* 1887. *Tim Smith*

1 Vestibule of andarun	4 Summer apartments	7 Entrances to basement
2 Winter apartments	5 Colonnade	8 Kitchen and service areas
3 Porches	6 Stair to terrace	9 Passage to men's quarters

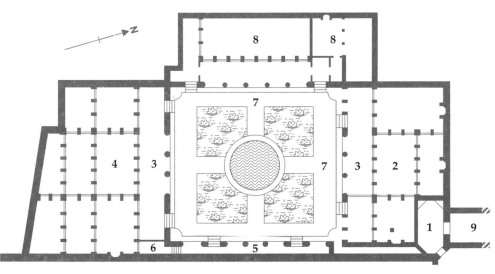

Street

39

the living quarters would ascend in wood. Special joinery was required to construct the graceful arched beams which supported each storey and to make the close-knit lattices which screened windows.

Comparable techniques were used in the construction of wooden *yalıs* found on the shores of the Bosphorus. Other materials included clay for roof tiles and paving for ground floors; brightly-coloured glass mosaic was set in the plaster frames which embellished the highest row of windows; and bronze and iron were used for gratings and gates. Brilliant polychrome tiles from the main production centres of Iznik and Kütahya were extensively used in Ottoman Turkish architecture from the sixteenth century onwards. Generally, however, their rich designs of flower and foliage scrolls were limited to interior decoration in mosques and in the grandest palaces and houses. They were only used externally as

Istanbul, panel of tiles from the palace of Fuad Pasha, mid-18th century.

Isfahan, frieze of tiles from interior of a palace, 17th century.

40

sudden splashes of colour, over doors and windows in the courtyards of mosques, and in panels and friezes on walls of colonnaded pavilions, to lighten the sombre grey or white background of the building. Colour also featured in the external appearance of homes. Both *konaks* and *yalıs* were traditionally painted a deep terracotta red. From the eighteenth century lighter shades of blue, yellow, green and pink were introduced.

The homes of Cairo were built to plans similar to those of the Istanbul *konak*, but the materials of stone, brick and wood were used in different proportions. Local limestone from quarries near Cairo was used for the deep blank wall of the ground floor, worked in neat rectangular blocks. The storeys above, together with their supporting arches, were built of dull red baked-clay bricks set in a mortar of straw, lime and rubble. This brick structure was then concealed with plaster and often painted with alternating bands of red ochre and white limewash. Wood was used for the shutters and windows of the closed balconies which projected into street and courtyard. These were fitted with lattices of carved and turned wood which in the intricacy and delicacy of their openwork designs were masterpieces of the joiner's craft. When newly built and freshly decorated the exterior of a rich Cairo home presented a surface of considerable textural impact.

Although brick was a major element in the architecture of Turkey and Egypt, it was essentially a foundation material usually, masked by stone facing or coats of plaster and paint. In Iran, however, brick was not only the principal building material but was treated as a decorative medium in its own right and combined with polychrome glazed tiles. From the seventeenth century the major religious buildings of Isfahan, Tehran, Shiraz

Iran, Mahan. Tiled dome of the shrine of Nimatullah Vali. 17th century.

Iran, mosaic tilework in the Gulestan Palace. Late 19th century.

and many provincial cities were immediately identifiable by their domes and courtyards swathed in turquoise, blue, white, yellow and green, worked in bold geometrical or graceful scrolling, foliage designs. The exteriors of the palaces and great households of Tehran show the same confident mingling of brick and tile. Building bricks were square, made of a yellow kiln-fired clay and sand mixture and worked up into neat courses bonded with a lime and sand mortar. The courses could be left unadorned, or patterned with motifs picked out in relief, such as bands and panels of intersecting stems and crosses.

Tilework provided an additional waterproof surface; it emphasized structure and added colour to offset the yellow of the bricks. Exterior walls were decorated in mosaic to produce geometrical designs in turquoise, white and yellow, or overglaze painting in a rich palette of pink, purple, yellow, shades of blue, green and orange. Mosaic tilework was ideal for vertical panels framing entrances and porches or horizontal friezes lining a courtyard, while overglaze painted tiles were made into spectacular floral panels resembling carpets and textile curtains, which were hung on walls and pediments. An especially lively development during the nineteenth century was the taste for large-scale narrative scenes in which poster-like images of heroes from popular literature mingled with scenes of contemporary life.

The colour of domestic building was further enriched by the use of stained glass mosaics of red, blue, emerald and yellow set within openwork wood panels used for fanlights and sliding sash windows. A comparatively sober element was introduced by the sparing use of stone. Panels of cream-coloured limestone or greenish marble were made into friezes running along the facades of the courtyards of both religious and domestic buildings, finely carved in shallow relief or openwork with graceful sprays of flowers.

3
THE HOME

> However simple their houses are on the outside, on the inside luxury and magnificence reign. Gold, rich fabrics, pearls and precious stones are there in an abundance of which it is difficult to convey an impression.

These observations by a Russian diplomat stationed in Istanbul relate to the houses of two great officials, the Grand Vizir (the Sultan's chief minister) and the Kaptan Pasha (supreme commander of the Ottoman fleet) and they vividly summarise the basic philosophy of interior decoration traditionally followed in the homes of the wealthy throughout the Middle East.

Home plans which often show great ingenuity and creativity in the orientation of rooms, courts, balconies, stairs and terraces had one dominating aim, to ensure that the interior space was efficiently used to create a private environment for family life. This is confirmed by Edward Lane's account of Cairo life of the early nineteenth century.

> In the plan of every house there is an utter want of regularity. The apartments are generally of different heights, so that a person has to ascend or descend one, two or more steps, to pass from one chamber to another adjoining it. The principal aim of the architect is to render the house as private as possible; particularly that part of it which is inhabited by the women; and not to make any window in such a situation as to overlook the apartments of another house.

Within the rules of strict segregation the interior was as comfortably and handsomely equipped and furnished as the family's means permitted, in effect to turn a house into a home, where a rich domestic culture could flourish. This took place in an environment which, by contemporary European standards, was remarkably empty of conventional furniture. Traditionally there were no suites of dining table, chairs and sideboards, beds, wardrobes and dressing tables. Furnishing consisted of cushions, covers, quilts. Apart from specific quarters such as stables, store rooms, kitchen and *hammams*, there was no real functional division between rooms. Even the main reception room of both the men's and women's quarters, although on a large scale and richly decorated, could equally be used as a dining and sleeping area. If there were large numbers of guests,

Istanbul, apartment in the palace of Esma Sultan. Thomas Allom, c1840

terraces, roofs, and even porches, were regarded as convenient places for sitting, eating and sleeping.

This concept of versatile space has both social and aesthetic significance. It supports the priority given to the family in Islamic culture. A flexibly organized home can offer accommodation and hospitality to all members and relations of an extended family. It has linguistic implications. In, for example, an early seventeenth-century Ottoman Turkish manual on architecture, the chapter listing types and parts of a building, takes a modular approach. Other than areas such as kitchens, bathrooms, treasuries or store-rooms of various kinds, rooms are described only according to location, climate and structural feature. There are upper-storey and lower-storey rooms, summer and winter rooms (sensible in view of the climatic conditions of the Middle East) rooms with flat, vaulted and domed roofs, inner and outer courts, and so on. Rooms for guests are specifically identified, indicating the importance of hospitality in Middle Eastern culture. In Turkish the word *selamlık* means both men's quarters and guest area.

Textiles provided the ideal means of combining spatial flexibility with the basic human need for ornament and colour. The cities of the Middle East had thriving textile industries which catered for domestic and export markets. Istanbul had workshops which produced luxurious fabrics and its markets stocked woven cloth from Bursa, Damascus and Aleppo. Bursa was itself famous for its opulent silks. Cairo had a flourishing market in linen and cotton, while Isfahan specialized in the manufacture of silks and block-printed cottons. Both Turkey and Iran produced woven and knotted pile carpets in wool and silk. The architecture of the Middle Eastern home needed such textiles to partition and adorn them. Hangings functioned as screens to divide halls and courtyards into manageable units. They served as curtains across doors and open colonnades. Textile design influenced architectural ornament. Repeated small checked and striped motifs in brickwork resembled weaving patterns. Panels of brilliantly coloured tilework, friezes of interlaced foliage and geometric motifs in carved and painted plaster and wood inlaid with ivory and mother-of-pearl could be effectively immobile textiles. The influence of textile design was so great that it was found in many of the objects used in a household. Ceramic bowls and jars were decorated with repeated and interlaced foliage motifs worked in combinations of cut and moulded techniques and brilliantly coloured glazes.

Within a household, textiles either directly as items of furnishing and dress or indirectly through the influence of their design on the decoration of ceilings, walls and floors, conveyed important messages about wealth, status within the family and community, personal taste and culture. Both the *selamlık* and *haremlik* of a grand residence were luxuriously decorated and equipped. The central reception hall was the largest and most lavishly ornamented room of the home. Sometimes the *selamlık* had the best rooms, sometimes they were of equal status. Much depended on the prestige and wealth of the family. A great official would require a large reception area to accommodate all his supplicants and guests.

Iran, Tabriz. Tile mosaic panels in the Blue Mosque, 1465.

Ceramic bowl painted with softly textured designs in underglaze colours. Iran, 14th century

The main reception area, as well as being the longest and widest room, was frequently the highest, flanked by two storeys of smaller rooms on each side connected by galleries and passages. In Istanbul and Cairo, one and sometimes two, sections of this room were raised above ground level and functioned as seating areas for the host and family where guests could be invited to join them. The room's interior was covered in decorated surfaces from ceiling to floor, in a unified style.

The reception rooms of both *selamlık* and *haremlik* of the wealthy of Istanbul mainly used wood, tilework and glass in their decorative schemes. Apart from the quarters of the Sultan and his family in the Topkapi Saray, where rooms and pavilions were roofed with domes and vaults covered with brilliant tilework, the ceilings of most houses were of wood treated in various ways. One of the most attractive treatments involved expert joinery, as cut wood was shaped and interlocked into a complex mosaic of star and diamond motifs, often grouped around a central boss carved into a rosette. When polished to a deep reddish brown these ceilings suggested warmth and comfort. By the nineteenth century, however, wooden ceilings were increasingly embellished with paint. Sections of the mosaic were picked out in contrasting colours, such as red and green, and outlined with gilding. Details, such as bunches of flowers and foliage scrolls, were also added.

Tiles painted with designs of vine scrolls and interlaced foliage. Iznik, 16th-17th century

Walls offered opportunities for colourful textured decoration where several materials and techniques could be combined. In the suites reserved for the Sultan and his mother in the *haremlik* of the Topkapi Saray, the walls of the reception rooms, of sixteenth to seventeenth century date, and of the pavilions in the terraced gardens of the fourth court, were panelled with tiles from the factories of Iznik. The tiles were painted in rich blue and turquoise on a white ground, all sealed under a lustrous colourless glaze. Designs of lotus and peony flowers rhythmically intertwine with curved leaves and resemble curtains and hangings. Alternating with them are panels and doors of dark wood inlaid in ivory and mother-of-pearl with meticulous interlocked geometrical motifs, a scheme which, again, suggests lengths of fabric. Other private apartments within the Topkapi Saray, of eighteenth century date, have reception rooms whose wood and plaster walls are charmingly decorated with panels of vases of flowers painted in a more naturalistic style.

The Topkapi Saray apartments set the highest decorative standards. In general, the walls of the homes of wealthy private citizens were decorated in wood and paint. A reception room would be lined with panels of wood inlaid and carved with geometrical motifs, alternating with cupboard doors and niches. Walls could be painted with graceful flower and foliage designs in clear fresh colours. From the late eighteenth century onwards, these designs were often replaced by panels of landscapes, showing the influence of European techniques of shading and perspective. This treatment of wall space was both practical and decorative. As interiors lacked freestanding furniture, cupboards and niches were used for the storage and display of clothes, soft furnishings

Istanbul, wall painted with flowers and fruit in 1709 in the apartments of Sultan Ahmet III in the Topkapi Saray.

and ornaments. These features were present in all rooms. In the reception rooms, however, a low *divan* of continuous seating lined the walls of the raised area. This and cupboards and niches were the only items of fitted immovable furnishing.

As the interior of the household had to be screened from the outside world, lower windows were covered with wooden shutters and strong lattices, which permitted control of the circulation of light and air. The upper level of windows, which also functioned as fanlights, gave scope for colour and design. These were filled with an intricate lacework of finely carved plaster worked into foliage, flowers and medallions, all filled with glass, richly coloured in emerald, deep blue, turquoise and amber yellow, which echoed the designs of tilework. By the late eighteenth to early nineteenth centuries, however, this heavy style of window decoration was increasingly replaced in the Bosphorus *yalıs* with plain glass screened by fabric blinds and curtains.

Floors varied according to the type and location of the household. The Istanbul climate is damp and chilly during the late autumn and winter months, which meant that floors, whether of stone or wood, were covered by carpets. The more open structures of the summer *yalı*, however, created the effect of an indoor garden. In the spacious reception rooms at ground level the floors were paved with polished slabs of marble, sometimes combined with black and white pebble mosaic worked with scrolling foliage designs, centred on a marble fountain. Lady Mary Wortley Montagu captures the charm of such rooms:

> But what pleases me best is the fashion of having marble fountains in the lower part of the room, which throw up several spouts of water, giving at the same time an agreeable coolness and a pleasant dashing sound, falling from one basin to another. Some of these fountains are very magnificent.

Households of the wealthy of Cairo enjoyed a comparable standard of decoration adapted to suit local taste and climate. Reception and family sitting rooms and, to a lesser extent, the smaller subsidiary rooms, had ceilings of wood laid as transverse beams which were usually painted and gilded. In the main rooms ceilings featured more elaborate geometrical patterns of intersecting stars, lozenges, hexagons painted in green, red and blue, and sometimes a high cupola was lit by insets of coloured glass. Wall facings varied according to the season and the means of the family. Generally they were plastered, whitewashed and then painted with designs of continuous repeated foliage and flowers. Occasionally walls were painted with views of religious sites; bands of inscriptions written in beautiful Arabic calligraphy were added. Reception rooms of the rich which were used during the hot summer months often had walls faced with panels of marble. As in traditional Ottoman Turkish homes the wall surface was divided by the intricately carved and inlaid wooden doors of cupboards, and niches which stored and displayed soft furnishings and ornaments. Deep

Cairo, interior of the house of Shaykh Sadat. Frank Dillon, c1875

Wooden panel with an intricate geometrical design made of inlaid units of carved wood and ivory. Cairo, 14th century

embrasures of the windows of closed projecting balconies, lined with carved wood panels and screened with intricate lattices, functioned as intimate small rooms. A continuous narrow wooden shelf running along the walls above the level of the windows was used for the display of fine ceramics and glass. Low stone or wood benches lined the walls of the seating areas at ground level. Windows in the upper rooms of a home of two storeys or more were filled with brightly-coloured glass and plaster mosaic in designs of geometrical motifs or bouquets of flowers. Possibly the most striking textural effect was reserved for the floors of reception rooms. These were paved with a mosaic of white and black marble and glazed red tile, patterned with chequered designs and interlocking radiating stars, like an elaborate patchwork composition. This combination of decoration and cool functional fittings was further enhanced by a small marble fountain in the centre from which water trickled into a shallow pool lined with a mosaic of delicate shell motifs.

The interiors of the great houses of Iran are distinctive for the way in which the apparently overwhelming impact of decoration in many techniques and colours is balanced by the open and spacious proportions of the buildings. A reception area encrusted with lavish ornament from ceiling to floor might open onto a colonnaded court simply decorated with monochrome brick patterns or white plaster. The more perceptive European visitors understood this balance of forms. Ella Sykes, on her way to Kerman in the late nineteenth century, notes that the traveller will:

> ... admire the skilful use made of plaster, ordinary-looking houses being beautified with stucco facades and imposing looking loggias supported on columns. Inside, the principal room will probably have an enormous window

Iran, Kashan. Interior of the house of the Borujerdi family, mid-19th century.

made of stained glass set in small leaded squares, the effect of the light streaming through and steeping the room in soft colours being very beautiful.

She also observed that luxurious decoration and furnishings were reserved for the *andarun*, the private quarters of the women and family. 'Here are sunk beds of flowers round the tank, which perhaps is lined with vivid blue tiles, and possibly, if the space be sufficient, a tree spreads its welcome shade in a corner of the enclosure.'

By the nineteenth century Iranian interior decoration comprised polychrome tile-work, carved, moulded and painted plaster, coloured glass and mirror mosaic, painting on wood and canvas, and created vivid textile effects blending with pictorial composition. Each technique was matched to the unit of a room's structure which would show it to best advantage. These principles applied equally to the Gulestan Palace, the country retreats of the court to the north of Tehran and to households of the more affluent in both Tehran, Isfahan and major provincial cities such as Shiraz and Kerman.

Tile painted in underglaze colours with the portrait of a tilemaker. In Nasiruddin Shah's summer palace at Sultanatabad completed in 1888.

Tile painted in a stippled and shaded underglaze black copied from a photograph of Nasiruddin Shah listening to a piano recital. From a frieze in the Gulestan Palace installed in 1887.

The predominant medium of decoration was polychrome ceramic tilework which had a long history as an essential feature of architecture in Iran. From the seventeenth century onwards, however, tiling exploded in a riot of design and colour over religious and secular buildings. By the nineteenth century tilework invaded every surface where it could find a space, draping the exterior and interior of buildings with friezes, hangings and borders. The main centres of tile production, namely Tehran, Isfahan and Shiraz, were kept busy catering to the fashion for tiles in interior decoration.

Semicircular pediments were placed over doors, narrow windows, and niches set in the upper half of a wall. European influences on interiors of the late nineteenth century introduced ornate fireplaces which offered still more space for tilework. A horizontal panel could be placed over a mantelpiece and a three-sided border of tiles could equally well decorate a door, window or fireplace. Many of these tiles, particularly from the 1880s onwards, were worked in the underglaze painted technique. This colourful technique encouraged the most lively and varied repertoire of subjects. Apart from the traditional themes of flowering scrolls and medallions, there were scenes from classical and romantic literature such as the ever-popular story of Yusuf and Zulaikha, landscape views, groups of European women and children in fashionable dress, and – perhaps the most interesting – interpretations in hatched and stippled monochrome black of contemporary photographs of Nasiruddin Shah in a variety of poses, such as listening to a piano recital or reviewing his troops. Tiles were also used to pave floors in repeated flower patterns or in zig-zag rippled motifs resembling watered silk.

Other decorative techniques matched tile-work in the inventiveness of their designs. Glass was used as in Istanbul and Cairo, made up into a mosaic of red, blue, green and yellow set within a wood frame and used for fanlights and sliding sash windows. A unique treatment of glass involved the use of a honeycomb mosaic of mirrorwork to create a spectacularly reflective surface on ceilings and vaults of both rooms and porches, which produced an intense silver light.

Friezes of repeated floral scrolls picked out in small pieces of coloured glass inlaid in a smooth white plaster ground, illustrate a more restrained use of glass. Carved, moulded and painted plasterwork has a long history in Iran as a form of architectural decoration. During the seventeenth century it was used in reception rooms to form rows of shaped niches to hold lamps. By the nineteenth century it had

Iran, carved stucco panels in the Bagh-i Firdaus (Garden of Paradise) a country house in the northern suburbs of Tehran, late 19th century.

Iran, Qazvin. A reception room in the house of the Amini family, mid-19th century.

Girl dancing with castanets. Attributed to Sayyid Mirza, c1840

developed into a highly elaborate means of decorating ceilings, walls and fireplaces, with designs in prominent relief of bouquets and bowls of flowers and fruit, among birds and garlands of foliage. Startling interior decoration was created with panels painted either directly onto plaster-coated walls or in oils onto canvas. Traditional schemes of flower and bird compositions mingled with large figurative subjects, handsome young men and beautifully dressed girls, placed in niches around a room. This style of painting scenes moved from walls to ceilings. One example was admired by Sir Frederick Goldsmid of the Persian Telegraph Department, who recalls the guest room of a house in the Caspian part of Enzeli in 1870:

> ... [The host] places at my disposal the traveller's room in his house, an apartment about 14 feet by 6, with pictures of flowers and females. A *décolléte* beauty on the ceiling is rouged up to the eyes and surrounded with miniatures of attendants in all kinds of impossible positions and attitudes, to say nothing of the flying charmers supporting her ...

Decoration of all these interiors was further enriched by textiles as many and fine as the family's financial and social position could afford. The use of curtains, hangings, covers, cushions and carpets could transform a room for changes in season and climate and for special occasions, a style which was flexible and practical. Small pieces of mobile furniture such as caskets for jewellery and personal effects, folding stands for books, metal and ceramic vessels for preparing and serving food, ornaments and luxuries such as flower vases, pages of calligraphy and finely illuminated manuscripts complemented the textiles.

In Turkey Lady Mary Wortley Montagu wrote in 1717 of the comfortably furnished

room in the *haremlik* which her wealthy hosts put at her disposal:

> ... the rooms are all spread with Persian carpets, and raised at one end (my chamber is raised at both ends) about two feet. This is the sofa, and is laid with a richer sort of carpet, and all around it a sort of couch, raised half a foot, covered with rich silk according to the fancy or magnificence of the owner. Mine is of scarlet cloth, with a gold fringe; round this are placed, standing against the wall, two rows of cushions, the first very large, and the next little ones; and here the Turks display their greatest magnificence. They are generally brocade, or embroidery of gold wire upon white satin:- nothing can look more gay and splendid. These seats are so convenient and easy, I shall never endure chairs as long as I live.

Surviving textiles of the period bear testimony to her vivid description. Velvets and heavy brocaded silks were woven in centres such as Istanbul, Bursa, Damascus and Aleppo to provide warmth and decoration in wealthy Ottoman households. Traditional colour-schemes based on deep crimson and green were enhanced by designs woven and embroidered in gold and silver thread, with bold stylized motifs of carnation, tulips and pine cones. Textiles were hung as curtains or decorative panels on walls and doors, used as screens to enclose areas in a large reception room, and made into cushions which could be combined and heaped in many formations for seating and reclining. A wide range of carpets with pile knotted in wool and silk covered the floors of reception and adjoining rooms. These were the products of Turkey's own centres such as Uşak and Gördes, and the much prized imports from Iran. There was a wide choice of design from angular foliate motifs, schemes quartered to resemble the layout of a formal garden, or spirals and scrolls of flowering stems entwined around medallions.

Velvet cushion cover embroidered with a design of stylized carnations. Turkey, 17th century

Opposite
Knotted wool carpet. Turkey, Usak, 17th century

59

Draped and carpeted rooms were versatile. They could easily be adapted for use as bedrooms. Bedding consisted of mattresses, padded quilts, pillows and sheets which were stored in the panelled and painted cupboards which lined the walls of a room: these were pulled out as needed and made up into flat beds on the floor carpet, often supported by cushions taken from the *divan*. Covers, napkins, towels and clothing were also stored in these cupboards. Covers were particularly flexible. Rich covers of embroidered and quilted silks and velvets were placed on seating areas for senior family members and important guests. Covers draped the mattresses and quilts of bedding and were also wrapped around bundles of clothing. If the textiles could be folded into small neat parcels they were wrapped in embroidered covers and stacked on open display in the niches and shelves of a room.

Mobile furniture was only used to supplement the textiles and to provide decoration. Wall niches and shelves held vases of flowers, and long-necked glasses with a single rose, carnation or tulip. There were folding stands made of wood, often lavishly decorated with ivory and mother-of-pearl inlay, which were opened out to hold books and manuscripts. Low stools were covered with metal trays to serve as tables at mealtimes. In some households carved wooden chests were also used for the storage of textiles and clothing.

Ceramic bowl and cover. Painted in underglaze colours with tulip and hyacinth sprays. Turkey, Iznik, late 16th century

A lion made up of Arabic calligraphy. Ink on paper within a marbled frame. An interpretation by Graham Day from an Ottoman Turkish original, 1988.

The main source of heat came from an ornate brass or copper lidded charcoal brazier which was moved about the room like a portable fireplace. It constantly needed replenishing. In extremely cold temperatures a table mounted over a metal bowl containing hot coals was brought in and covered with a large quilt which could be drawn up over the knees of the family and their guests. Apart from natural daylight which filtered through stained glass and window lattices, or streamed into open courtyards and porches, lighting was supplied by candles and oil lamps which at best created flattering contrasts of light and shadow.

Personal possessions added an individual character to private space. Brightly-coloured local Iznik pottery was used together with imported Chinese blue and white porcelain, for both flower vases and bowls for sweets. Rosewater sprinklers were of local or Venetian glass. Depending on means and taste, ewers and basins, soap dishes, incense containers and candlesticks were of gold or silver.

Beautifully written and decorated manuscripts of the *Qur'an*, pages of calligraphy and illustrated editions of literary classics were commissioned by wealthy patrons for study and enjoyment within their households. These were cased in leather bindings embossed, stamped and coloured with medallion motifs. The patterns on such bindings resemble those of the formal designs found in embroidered silk covers and knotted pile carpets.

In the reception rooms of both *selamlık* and *haremlik* there were sets of metal coffee pots, porcelain cups in filigree holders, and small dishes for offering coffee and refreshments to guests. Accessories and ornaments indicated the separate nature of male and female quarters. Carved wooden brackets, often painted or inset with mother-of-pearl, were hung among the cupboards and niches of the *selamlık* rooms. The brackets held the elaborately folded turbans worn by upper-class Ottoman Turkish men. Their other personal possessions might include lavishly embroidered leather and velvet wallets to contain identity documents and letters, coin purses and pipes.

By contrast, within the *haremlik* rooms, jewellery and accessories were kept in lavishly decorated caskets often of embossed and stamped silver, and in painted boxes and chests. Women's possessions included objects for personal grooming: silver mirrors, combs, soap bowls, small pots and boxes to hold cosmetics, and high-heeled clogs worn in the bath. There were frames and baskets of needles and thread for the embroidery which was a major domestic art. There were also pen boxes, sets of brushes and pens, paper, and instruments such as the long-necked saz and lute, for women who were gifted in the arts of calligraphy and music.

Slowly, changes took place in the treatment of the interiors of households of the rich, through contact with European styles of furnishing. Beginning modestly with imported glass lamps, ewers and dishes from Bohemia, pieces of furniture were introduced which more narrowly defined the functions of rooms. Melek Hanim, writing of her reception in the guest suite of the palace of Esma Sultan in 1848 describes this stylistic evolution clearly. Her apartments:

> ... consisted of three rooms – drawing room, bedroom and dining room. Roses, white and red, adorned the walls; the curtains were of beautiful striped cashmere; costly carpets covered the floors; splendid mirrors were arranged at intervals; golden cups enriched with precious stones, and filled with sweetmeats, were placed here and there ... Besides comfortable divans, there were arm-chairs of European manufacture, and lamps were disposed together with large massive candlesticks in the Oriental style, resembling those used for tapers in the churches of France...

The wealthy in Cairo also furnished their homes with handsome textiles, though in a different way. The use of carved wooden lattice screens across the wide and deep windows left no space for velvet and brocaded silk hangings and curtains, which in any case would have been too thick and heavy for the Cairo climate. Floors were paved with an elaborate mosaic in a variety of coloured marble which provided pattern and colour. Small carpets did, however, offset the chill of stone underfoot during the winter months and also functioned as informal seating. Textiles were mainly used both for the

Silver toilet service - jewellery box, comb and hair ornament, mirror, soap dish and bath clogs. Made by Manuk Güllüdere in Istanbul to traditional designs, 1990-92.

A party at dinner or supper. Cairo, 1830s

Opposite
Iran, silk cover lavishly embroidered with
scrolling and intertwined foliage and flower
designs, 18th-19th century

cushions which decorated the low benches lining the walls of reception rooms and for the bedding which, as in Turkey, was stored in cupboards until required. Mobile pieces of furniture were, if anything, fewer than in Turkish houses, consisting of low stools on which a metal tray was placed to serve as a table at mealtimes, and charcoal-burning braziers to warm the room in cases of extreme cold. Ceramic vases and the personal possessions of the household, on the continuous wooden shelf above window level, added an element of individual character. As in Turkey, changes were introduced, especially after the modernization programmes of the 1870s which transformed Cairo. Luxurious European-style decoration and furniture as described by Ellen Chennells, governess to Princess Zeyneb, daughter of the Khedive Ismail, transformed the homes of the rich:

> We were in a spacious saloon, richly furnished in the French style, lined with looking-glasses, couches, sofas and chairs, covered with yellow damask satin, hangings of the same at the windows, and numerous doors that led from this saloon into inner apartments; making it cool and pleasant in summer, but rather draughty in winter. Rich thick carpets on the ground, large lustres hung from the ceiling, and girandoles from the walls.

In Iran there were specific means for creating the functional versatility of rooms, including the distinction between men's and women's quarters. These varied in practice from those found in Turkish and Egyptian households. In homes where the *biruni* and *andarun* consisted of apartments around a rectangular or square courtyard, sash windows with wooden frames extending from ceiling to floor could be raised or lowered at will to divide or extend a living space, and to open or to close areas according to

64

65

seasonal weather conditions. The absence of both fitted and movable furnishing was remarkable. There was no equivalent of the raised Turkish and Egyptian *divan* seating around the walls. There were no small stands to hold metal trays for food. Recessed niches in the walls provided a surface for books and ornaments such as ceramic or glass vases of flowers. There were sometimes chests for the storage of household textiles and clothing, although these could be neatly stacked at the back of a room and covered with a fine cloth. Thin mattresses and padded quilts arranged on the floor provided bedding. Meals were served on a cloth spread out on the floor. The use of more structured seating arrangements was confined to court life. Fath Ali Shah Qajar was painted and described seated in the formal audience vestibule of the Gulestan Palace on a large wide marble throne supported on the shoulders of sculpted figures, but this is exceptional. The simplicity of floor-level life meant that rooms could be easily transformed into sleeping, eating and reception areas.

The most important textiles, therefore, in Iranian domestic culture were floor coverings, mainly a family's collection of carpets with a knotted pile in wool and silk. Variations in the depth and thickness of the pile meant that carpets could be used as comfortable and warm floor coverings or as covers for pillows and cushions. Different types of carpet had specific functions and not all of a family's collection were on display at any one time. They were carefully grouped and placed over a protective felt underlay which was a decorative textile in its own right. Dr Wills of the Persian Telegraph Department, one of the most accurate observers of traditional Iranian culture, describes this arrangement in a wealthy home of the 1860s:

> The namad or felts (carpets) are generally used by Persians to go round the room and act as a frame to the carpet (kali) which occupies the top and centre. They are three in number for each room; two kanareh, or side pieces, a yard to a yard and a half wide, and a sir-andaz, literally that which is thrown over the head (of the apartment). The kanareh are from half to two and a half inches in thickness, and are usually of a light-brown or yellow-ochre colour, being ornamented with a slight pattern of blue and white, or red and green, which is formed by pinches of coloured wool inserted when the felt is made.

There were carpet designs to suit all tastes, woven in the city workshops of Kashan, Isfahan and Kerman. In general, however, the preferred choice was for exuberant floral patterns to harmonize with the lavish interior decoration. They included palmettes, bouquets of flowers entwined within foliage and ribbon swirls and scrolls, alternating stripes of flowers and leafy stems, formal arrangements of medallions, as well as directional designs such as trees laden with flowers and fruit. Colours matched the richness of the designs, with motifs in deep brick and crimson reds, golden orange and yellow, light and dark blues and greens displayed against a background of beige or creamy white. All

Knotted wool carpet with a tree design also found in tilework decoration on monuments ranging in date from 1829 to 1900. Iran, Qum, c1960

of these carpet designs reveal a strong affinity to tilework and to carved and painted plaster-work. It is therefore not at all surprising that a taste for large-scale pictorial designs began to develop during the nineteenth century.

Traditional literature and foreign prints, engravings and photographs provided subjects for the carpets. In a society which enjoyed large oil paintings of handsomely dressed men and women there was nothing inconsistent in a taste for pictorial carpets which were woven with great technical dexterity and extremely fine knotting. Subjects included scenes of court entertainment with musicians and dancers, flowering trees with exotic creatures such as the mongoose and duck-billed platypus perched on their branches among lions and nightingales.

Many textile fabrics and techniques were resourcefully exploited to provide drapery to supplement floor coverings. Silks in white and yellow were quilted and embroidered in fine silk threads of crimson, pink, blue and green, using a neat chain stitch to outline and fill designs of medallions against a field of flower motifs, all contained within a border of deeply curved floral scroll. These quilts were used as bedcovers or as floor-level seating. A more sumptuous treatment of embroidery is seen in covers of crimson silk velvet worked in coloured silks and silver thread, with designs of flowers and birds often enfolding panels of inscription.

Although textiles were mainly used as covers there is evidence that they also functioned as hangings and curtains. Dr Wills notices in a Tehran house of the 1860s that 'The doors, which were of polished walnut-wood, were covered by curtains of bright colours of Yezd silk, some six feet by four, simply suspended in front of them.' Hangings and curtains provided splendid displays of skill and design; certain towns of Iran were famous for their specialized products. Kerman was renowned during the eighteenth and nineteenth centuries for its flourishing textile industry which catered for furnishing and clothing needs with a wide range of woven fabrics and knotted pile carpets. A distinctive embroidered textile was also produced, usually of fine red wool with lively designs of foliate stems and medallions, birds and cypress trees worked in neat outline and flat filling stitches to simulate the texture of weaving. The Caspian town of Resht specialized in the intricate and time-consuming technique of embroidered patchwork. A mosaic of closely-woven wool pieces in strong reds, greens, yellows and black was stitched together and embellished with appliqué and embroidered detail in contrasting colours. Subjects ranged from symmetrical arrangements of foliage to ambitious pictorial compositions with figures.

Block-printed cotton was a versatile fabric used for curtains, hangings, bedcovers and also clothing. This fabric, a speciality of Isfahan, was printed with carved wooden blocks to produce an outline in black which was then filled in with red, blue and yellow. The designs were both versatile and imaginative. Large pictorial compositions based on trees

Wool hanging finely embroidered with birds and medallions among foliage. Iran, Kerman, 19th century

69

Carved wooden blocks used in fabric printing. Iran, Isfahan, late 19th century

Page from a book of pattern samples for fabric printing. India, Madras, 1859

with tigers and peacocks, figurative scenes and hunting expeditions were used for hangings and curtains; while small repetitive floral designs were preferred for clothing.

Utensils, ornaments and personal possessions which completed the furnishing of the Iranian interior matched decoration and textiles in their form and style. Ceramic bowls, dishes and jugs were made of a fine-textured white clay mixture and were painted with flower and foliage designs in either monochrome blue or mixed with green, yellow, red and black and sealed with a transparent colourless glaze. Imports of Chinese porcelains decorated with crowded fussy designs in *famille rose* enamels, and wares from European factories, such as Wedgewood, Minton and Sèvres were also popular. Finely engraved brass was fashioned into ornate candlesticks, covered bowls and occasional pieces such as peacocks. Fireplaces were introduced into Iranian houses through European influence. The mantelpiece was a convenient focus for rows of vases, brass lamps, gilt-framed mirrors and coloured prints.

The craft of painted papier mâché was used in Iran to fashion a great range of practical and decorative objects for the home. The painting is closely related to manuscript

Ceramic pipe base, painted in underglaze blue and overglaze polychrome colours with a fashionably dressed rider in a flowering landscape. Iran, Isfahan, 17th century

70

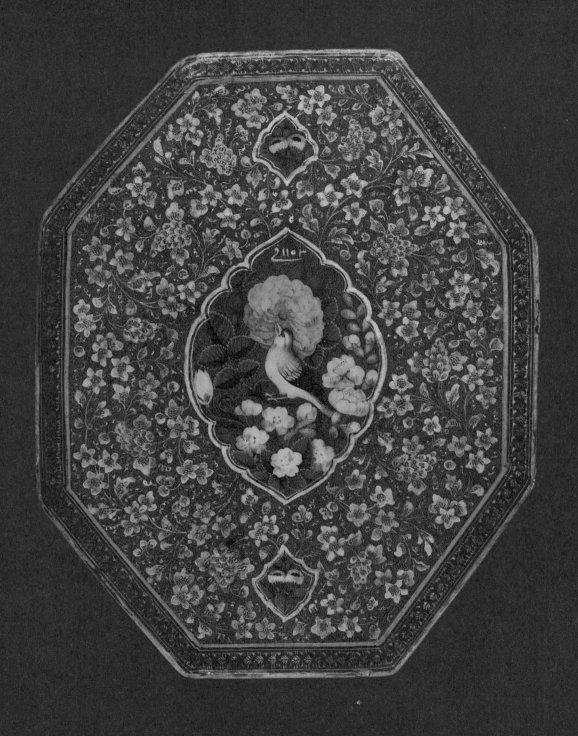

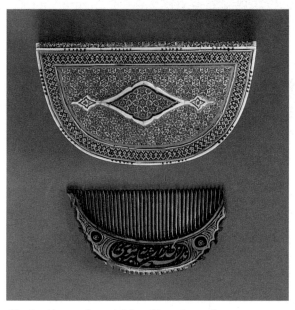

Candlestick of copper coated with silver. Finely engraved with complex figure scenes. Iran, 19th century

Comb with case of mosaic inlay of ivory in wood. Iran, Shiraz, 19th century

illustration, with designs meticulously outlined and painted in watercolours and then sealed with layers of transparent resinous varnish. Papier mâché was made into caskets for the storage of jewellery and documents, book covers, pen cases, trays for pins and trinkets, and mirror cases. One of the most appealing features of their decoration is the subject matter. As well as the favourite Yusuf and Zulaikha, exquisitely detailed studies of flowers and lively views of everyday life were popular. They offer, in miniature, a revelation of the values and customs of Iranian domestic life and culture.

Papier mâché was complemented by the equally meticulous craft of mosaic inlay work which decorated objects ranging from door panels, screens and boxes to personal accessories such as comb and mirror cases. The technique involves gluing strips of bone, ivory and coloured woods together in clusters to form design units. Layers are then cut from these blocks and glued to the wood base of the object and sanded and sealed with a transparent varnish. The finished designs are based on intricate geometrical motifs such as hexagons and stars. Eventually European-style furniture entered the households of the Qajar rulers, their court and wealthy subjects, especially after Nasiruddin Shah's reconstruction of Tehran during the 1860s-70s. Their ornate late Victorian style blended effortlessly into the rich Iranian interior.

Painted papier mâché mirror case. A delicate design of a nightingale among roses. Iran, Shiraz. Signed Ashraf and dated 1740 AD (1153 H)

4
HOME LIFE

On 12 January 1849, Lady Sheil, wife of the British Minister to the Court of Iran:

> [I am] now prepared to pay my respects to the Serkar e Madar e Shah, her Highness the Shah's mother. The Shah's mother is handsome, and does not look more than thirty, yet her real age must be at least forty. She is very clever, and is supposed to take a large share in the affairs of the government. She also has the whole management of the Shah's anderoon; so that I should think she must have a good deal to occupy her mind, as the Shah has three principal wives...

These observations hint at the complex nature of family life within the great households of the privileged and wealthy members of Middle Eastern society. This life, traditionally based on a network of kinship ties, relationships through marriage and obligations to dependents, required a large extended house in order to function effectively. Normally two or three generations lived in the same home. The family structure was officially patriarchal, with the senior male member of the household having ultimate authority over the others. A home of the rich would usually accommodate the father, his wife or wives, married sons and their families, single sons, unmarried or divorced daughters and a retinue of attendants and servants. There were, naturally, variations to this pattern depending on financial means and individual circumstances. A widowed grandmother could live in her grandson's home in a suite of rooms allocated to her. This was normal practice among upper-class Turks. Among the most affluent, sons and daughters had establishments provided for them. Sultan Ahmet III had built in 1718 on the shores of the Bosphorus a luxurious residence for his daughter Fatma. The Khedive Ismail in the 1870s organized similar accommodation for his sons in Cairo. The family unit was organic and flexible, often incorporating relatives such as widowed and divorced sisters of the head of the household, and cousins in

Painted papier mâché bookcover. Ladies at a party.
Iran, mid-19th century

varying degrees of relationship, as charity to those in reduced circumstances was both a social and a religious obligation.

There was one convention, however, which was carefully observed whatever the size and means of the extended family: the segregation of men and women. This had evolved through a combination of long-established Middle Eastern custom and Islamic recommendations for modest behaviour. It was expressed in the strict division of a household into separate quarters and in the association of men with public and women with private life respectively. This influenced the allocation and planning of space within houses and also had social and cultural implications. The terms used for the men's quarters, *selamlık* in Turkish, *mandara* in Arabic and *biruni* in Persian, all relate to greeting, openness and the outside world. They stress the men's quarters as a place of reception of unrelated as well as related male guests which included business associates and foreign visitors.

Although the head of the household and other men could eat and sleep and spend much of their leisure time in these quarters, there was no underlying concept of home. They were not, in any circumstances, visited by the women of the family. In Turkish, the word *selamlık*, literally 'place of greeting', was applied to any reception hall where formal audience was given; the occasion rather than the place was significant. It was also used to identify the ceremony of the Sultan's attendance at the mosque on Friday.

In contrast, the women's apartments were better defined as a home. All the related females of a household lived there, together with children and servants. Access was strictly limited to the head of the household and to male members and close relations of the family who could live and sleep there. Again the terms used were significant. The Arabic word *harim* and Turkish *haremlik* both imply a forbidden, sacred, secluded area while the Persian *andarun* simply means the inside place.

Harem also described and had a bearing on the role of the women themselves. Their sphere of activity was mainly confined to the seclusion of the home. When they went out they discreetly enveloped themselves in all-concealing robes and veils thus maintaining their segregation.

Within the house, the custom of polygamy added further complexity to the structure of domestic life, as Islam permits, but does not necessarily recommend, a limit of four legal wives, all of whom must be treated equally. Outside the rigidly organized hierarchies of the *harems* of the Ottoman Sultans and the Shahs of Iran, which were obviously exceptions, there were other ways of organizing the demands of the household.

Wives could live in the same home but in separate suites of rooms within the *harem*, each with her own children and attendants. This situation explains the complex architecture of some traditional homes in Cairo, where the *harem* is a cumulative maze of individual units, loosely grafted together. Relationships were easier in a household built on a grand scale. In Cairo of the 1870s three of the Khedive Ismail's wives lived with him

Istanbul, ladies' excursion in an araba. *Count Amadeo Preziosi, 1853*

76

in the Abdin Palace. They all had their own magnificent suites of apartments and, according to European women who met them, such as Ellen Chennells, governess to the Khedive's daughter Princess Zeyneb, the women lived amicably together. An alternative solution was to maintain separate establishments. This seemed preferable in both Egypt and Turkey. For example, the Khedive Ismail's fourth wife lived in a separate palace with her son, Tewfik Pasha, the heir-apparent, but she joined the other wives at formal ceremonies. Whichever solution was chosen, polygamy was a costly business requiring tact and understanding as well as considerable financial resources and it was not universally practised.

It would be inaccurate to assume, however, that because women had defined private roles, they were without influence, at least in upper-class and middle-class society. Segregation meant that the senior women supervised the domestic management of the *harem*. Lady Sheil noted how powerful the mother of Nasiruddin Shah was. The Valide Sultan, mother of a reigning Ottoman Sultan, exercised comparable power over his *haremlik*, and had real political control through the patronage and influence which this position brought. As Muslim women could own property, many administered directly or through agents, homes, orchards and shops in the bazaar quarters. They often invested their revenues in further commercial ventures or charitable bequests.

Life within the home was also shaped by Muslim religious practice. Practising Muslims pray five times a day and the times for prayers, spaced throughout the day, frame a family's routine. Muslim prayer is flexible, as it may be performed anywhere, and it conditions daily life through integration rather than disruption. The great city mosques are accessible all day, but the small mosques of a residential quarter normally open only for the midday prayer and for special religious celebrations. Prayers generally took place at home, as individual or family acts of devotion, and in the workplace. Men would take part in public prayer, usually the noon prayers in the mosque, which on Fridays was replaced by congregational prayer accompanied by a sermon. Women prayed at home, or if they went to the mosque, in an area or balcony specially reserved and screened for them. Within the home, space allocated to prayer varied, as only the wealthiest families could afford a small private mosque.

As the requirements for prayer were knowledge of the direction facing Mecca, access to water for the ritual ablutions, and a mat on which to kneel, praying could take place in any room. Despite this simplicity, families would include among their household textiles small knotted pile carpets or beautifully embroidered cloths which served as prayer mats.

All the family would rise early in time for the morning prayer, between dawn and sunrise. After dressing and breakfast they were ready for the day's activities. Men either left for their work or moved to the *selamlık* to receive guests and business associates, so domestic culture was the responsibility of the women, who supervised household maintenance and spent most of their leisure time in the *haremlik*.

As in all pre-industrial societies housework was laborious and time-consuming. Fortunately a wealthy householder could afford to employ a large retinue of servants to

Embroidered linen napkins. Turkey, 19th-20th century

perform both general and specialized tasks. The main work consisted of dusting, sweeping and washing the apartments, laundering clothing and textiles, and arranging food supplies. Dusting and sweeping, using brushes and brooms of split reeds bound at one end and without handles, were endless and back-breaking jobs. Marble floors were cleaned with sponges. Ella Sykes sums up the problems of housework in Kerman in the late nineteenth century:

> The floors of the rooms were made of beaten mud, like the whole house, and although they were covered with felts, over which striped cotton floor cloths were spread, yet we were never free from dust; and a careful attention to the clearing out of corners was imperative, if we did not wish to be overrun with tarantulas or scorpions.

Laundrywork was limited to the clothing and textiles that could be easily washed and ironed, such as undergarments, sheets, pillowcases, napkins and towels. Elaborately decorated garments and textiles, such as those embroidered or woven with metallic thread, were regularly brushed and aired and stored wrapped in protective covers. Shopping for food for a large household was another major task requiring considerable skill in identifying reliable sources of good, fresh, produce. Going to market was a daily activity entrusted to experienced servants. Cooking oils, preserved meats, fish, pickled and dried fruit and vegetables, nuts, rice and flour were stored for the autumn and winter months. Plenty of fresh fruits and vegetables were available in spring and summer, while certain districts were famous for the excellence of their produce, such as the yoghurt of the Bosphorus suburb of Kanlıca, the sweet melons of Meshed and the pistachio nuts of Rafsanjan in Iran.

Once the basic needs of housekeeping had been dealt with there was a choice of activity which combined both duty and leisure. A major responsibility was the supervision and education of the many children and young people, both relatives and dependents of a great household. Children were desired, valued and treated with much love and attention, and brought up in the *harem*. Their early training in language and the practices of Islam was, therefore, acquired from their mothers and female relations who kept the regard and affection of their children throughout their lives. Together with loving and indulgent care, children were also educated in social graces and respect for older people, parents and other family members. At its best, such an upbringing led to an impressive combination of humanity and courtesy.

Beyond these fundamentals education varied according to means, social status and talent. Royal children were educated entirely by specialist instructors within the palace system. Otherwise education could be at home or at school. This applied to both boys and girls, as segregation was not imposed until about the age of seven. Children would therefore receive formal instruction in reading and writing, and study of the *Qur'an* either through hired tutors or at a primary school attached to the local mosque. After the age of seven, boys continued to study through graded schools and institutions attached to the great mosques if they wished to pursue a career in the legal or religious establishment. They would also take a more active part in the life of the *selamlık* where they developed their social and diplomatic skills among their father's guests.

Iran, Qur'an *case of finely engraved brass. Iran, dated 1707*

Opposite
Boys climbing trees watched by their tutor. Iran, Isfahan, 17th century

The education of girls, although confined to the inner space of the *haremlik*, was more varied than has been commonly supposed. They were trained in household management, including the supervision of the many servants, sewing, embroidery and cooking. Most of them understood the principles of Islam and could recite parts of the *Qur'an*. In the palaces and in the wealthiest and most scholarly households, they were literate and studied Arabic, Persian and Turkish literature, and music with private tutors. This pattern also enabled the daughters of the rich to expand their horizons. By the late nineteenth century, European governesses were engaged to teach them French and English. They did not, however, employ their accomplishments in the public domain until changing social conditions enabled them to work outside the home.

In addition to these intellectual pursuits, girls and women spent much of their time in sewing and embroidery. In a domestic culture which relied so much on textiles for furnishing this was an essential task. Some textiles, such as the velvets embroidered in gold and silver thread and block-printed cottons and muslins were professional work and were brought into the home by merchants and pedlars.

Girls were trained in needlework from an early age and spent much of their time working on textiles for their family households and for the trousseau which a bride was obliged to take to her new home. Thus a steady supply of sheets, towels, quilts, napkins, covers for pillows, turbans, food trays and prayer mats was ensured through all this female industry. In well-staffed households, the senior lady supervised production and taught the girls. Plain sewing was done by maidservants, while fine embroidery was the province of daughters and some specially trained attendants. Standards were high and gave an outlet for the display of technical skill and creative talent. Embroidery was also a means of generating some independent income, as Edward Lane observed in Cairo of the 1830s:

> Many women, even in the houses of the wealthy, replenish their private purses by ornamenting handkerchiefs and other things in this manner, and employing a 'dellaleh' (or female broker) to take them to the market, or to other hareems, for sale.

There were considerable regional variations in fabric, stitch and design but the most extensive use of embroidery was found among the Ottoman Turks, who embellished every textile surface with imaginative designs worked in a combination of drawn-thread and running stitches in intense or subtly-shaded silks. Lady Mary Wortley Montagu's letter to Lady Mar of 10 March, 1718 sums up the quality of the table linens:

> The knives were of gold, the hafts set with diamonds, but the piece of luxury that grieved my eyes was the table cloth and napkins, which were all tiffany, embroidered with silks and gold in the finest manner in natural flowers. It was with the utmost regret that I made use of these costly napkins, as finely wrought as the finest handkerchiefs that ever came out of this country. You may be sure that they were entirely spoilt before dinner was over.

Dress traditions were ideally suited to the display of textiles as the conditions of both climate and social convention required that the human form be draped and swathed in layers of fabric. Dress was a major preoccupation among men and women in Middle

Eastern society, notably among the élite. It was one of the most powerful signals of a person's status in both the public world and in the private domain of family life.

The importance of dress was indicated by the choice of fabrics available, from the costly silk brocades and velvets woven in exclusive workshops for use at the court of Sultan and Shah, to the silks, wools, cottons and linens of both local and foreign manufacture which were sold in the bazaars, or brought to great households for inspection before purchase. While the elaborate uniforms and robes were made by specialist tailors, most of the family's clothes were made at home. Emine Foat Tugay charmingly describes the practices of an early twentieth-century Ottoman household:

> In spring and autumn bales of printed cotton or of flannelette would arrive at our house to be made up into dresses for the maids and kalfas. The former were dressed alike, but the kalfas and bacis were allowed to choose their own materials and style. A Greek seamstress who lived in the neighbourhood took possession of the sewing room and, assisted by maids who were clever with their needles, undertook the task of clothing the female staff. Each maid received four cotton dresses for the summer, two for work and two for the afternoons, and four made of flowered flannelette, as well as a woollen dress for the winter.

This routine essentially was followed in preceding centuries before the introduction of mass-produced clothing.

Upper-class women spent much time and effort on their wardrobes and accessories, as the maintenance of an elegant and bejewelled appearance reinforced the status of their families. Dress styles were distinguished by combinations of richly-patterned fabrics,

Photograph of Kopses, companion to Princess Zeyneb, daughter of the Khedive Ismail, taken in Cairo in 1873.

Woman's jacket of block-printed cotton. Iran, late 19th century

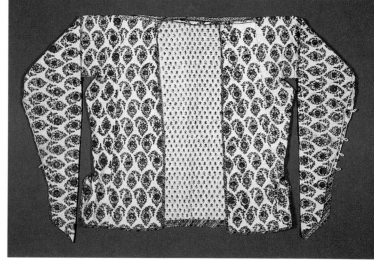

which allowed full scope for personal taste. Court fashions set the standards for Istanbul and all major cities of the Ottoman Empire. Garments were gracefully combined and accessorized, beginning with a long-sleeved chemise of white, finely-pleated silk gauze or linen edged with a fine-knotted lace. Over this, voluminous trousers, long neatly-fitting robes with trailing divided skirts and sometimes a short tight jacket were worn. Fabric, colour and texture included silks patterned with bold flower motifs, narrow vertical stripes, or plain silks in embroidered gold and silver thread all in strong colours of crimson, green, and purple. Elaborately jewelled belts or swathed shawls encircled the waist. Many embroidered and lace-edged scarves were intricately wrapped around the head to form a turban.

Embroidered velvet slippers or heelless mules were worn indoors. Quantities of bracelets, earrings and pendants were added, with brooches pinned to the headdress. Equally spectacular hairdressing and cosmetics completed the look. Hair was plaited into many braids, often entwined with strings of jewellery. Faces and lips were powdered and rouged, eyes were outlined with black kohl, eyebrows plucked and darkened, and henna stained nails, hands and feet. Lady Mary Montagu writing in 1718 describes the results of all this effort:

> She was dressed in a caftan of gold brocade, flowered with silk, very well fitted to her shape and showing to advantage the beauty of her bosom, only shaded by the thin gauze of her shift. Her drawers were pale pink, her waistcoat green and silver, her slippers white, finely embroidered, her lovely arms adorned with bracelets of diamonds and her broad girdle set round with diamonds; upon her head a rich Turkish handkerchief of pink and silver, her own fine black hair hanging a great length in various tresses, and on one side of her head some bodkins of jewels.

Comparable styles were worn by upper-class women of Cairo who were much influenced by mainstream Ottoman fashions. Their counterparts in Iran, with equally

Silk velvet woven with a classic design of three dots among double waves. Turkey, late 15th-16th century

Girl's robe of striped silk. Turkey, 18th century

Woman's jacket and trousers of gold brocaded silk.Iran, early - mid 19th century

striking jewels and make-up, by the nineteenth century favoured a bell-shaped outline. Over a fine gauze chemise they wore short, tight jackets, fitting snugly to the waist, and either a gathered ankle-length skirt or voluminous flaring trousers, all made in stiff silk brocade, with a headdress consisting of a neat cap studded with precious stones or a modest shawl tightly framing the face. The full costume had considerable impact and provocative charm, as Lady Sheil's account of Nasiruddin Shah's mother reveals:

> The Shah's mother was dressed with great magnificence. She wore a pair of trousers made of gold brocade. These Persian trousers are always, as I have before remarked, very wide, each leg being, when the means of the wearer allow it, wider than the skirt of a gown, so that they have the effect of an exceedingly ample petticoat; and as crinolines are unknown, the elegantes wear ten and eleven pairs of trousers, one over the other in order to make up for the want of the above important invention. But to return to the Shah's mother: her trousers were edged with a border of pearls embroidered on braid; she had a thin blue crepe chemisette, also trimmed with pearls... A small jacket of velvet was over the chemisette, reaching to the waist, but not made to close in front, and on the head a small shawl, pinned under the chin. On the shawl were fastened strings of large pearls and diamond sprigs; her arms were covered with handsome bracelets, and her neck with a variety of costly necklaces.

All this splendour was strictly reserved for indoor wear. Outdoor clothing varied according to region. Women in Istanbul wore a long, dark coat and concealed their heads and faces under the two scarves of the *yaşmak*, while Cairene and Iranian women were covered from head to toe in cloaks, and masked their faces with long rectangular veils.

While the division between private and public space continued to be strictly observed in dress convention, the impact which European practices had upon town planning and architecture also influenced fashion. Gradually European styles penetrated the *haremlik* of the élite of Istanbul and Cairo, where traditional garments gave way to tailored fashions. These were imported from Paris and Vienna for the princesses of the Ottoman Sultan's and Khedive's households, while others had to manage with copies sewn by enterprising Levantine dressmakers. This sartorial European influence was paralleled in the clothing of male courtiers and officials, whose traditional robes and turbans were replaced by suits of frock coats and narrow trousers and a fez or black lambskin hat.

Cooking and serving meals were essential and highly-rated activities. A remarkable food culture had evolved in the Middle East, distinguished for making the best use of fresh ingredients subtly seasoned with herbs and spices to enhance rather than drown

Women in outdoor dress. Iran, late 19th century

Photograph of Prince Ibrahim and Princess yneb, children of the Khedive Ismail, taken in Cairo in 1873.

Opposite
Portrait of Sultan Ahmet I (1603-17). Turkey, 17th century

flavours, and for combinations of dishes which provided balanced and varied meals. Dietary rules were practical and simple. Pork was forbidden as much for hygienic as religious reasons. Foods to be served cold were cooked in olive oil rather than butter which would turn rancid; milk was processed into yoghurt and cheese. Meals were prepared in kitchens located between the *selamlık* and *haremlik* or in separate outhouses, depending on the size of the house and its grounds. All major households employed cooks to cater both for everyday needs and for special occasions.

Meal-times fitted in with the daily ritual of prayer and made the best use of daylight hours. Breakfast therefore was taken immediately after the dawn prayer. The main meal of the day, family supper, was usually served in the late afternoon or after sunset prayer. By current European standards, meals were relatively informal in their location and service. There was no specific dining area, since all rooms in a traditional household were flexible. In Ottoman Turkey and Egypt a large tray was brought into a room and set on a low stool or stand to serve as a table, around which the diners sat on the floor, each equipped with a napkin. In Iran a cloth was spread out on the floor. Food was brought in on covered trays and served on metal plates or large flaps of bread, and eaten with the right hand. The only utensils used were serving ladles, scoops and soup spoons.

Dishes were either set out together, regardless of ingredients, or served in quick succession. This style of service was followed at all social levels, only differing for the royal courts and the wealthy in degree and quality of the textiles, utensils and ingredients. Only with the introduction of European fashions during the nineteenth century, were meals in upper-class households served at tables with place settings and a menu of several courses.

Breakfast was a simple and light meal eaten quickly before the family separated for the daily routine. It consisted of bread, cheese, yoghurt, seasonal fruits and tea. Variations included eggs, homemade jams, and in Egypt a bowl of *ful medammes* - a substantial stew of brown fava beans served with olive oil and cumin.

Preparations for supper started in the afternoon after the noon prayer and a snack lunch (which usually consisted of leftovers). Cooking for supper was a serious business. Catering was for family, servants, and also for distribution to the poor and needy at the mosque. Dishes in wealthy households consisted of soups, meat, fish and vegetables, staples of rice and bread, and seasonal fruits, and all were made with distinctive regional variations. Soups generally had a vegetable and lentil base, but in Iran were enriched with dried fruits and pomegranate juice. Meats were lamb, occasionally venison in Iran, and poultry, grilled, roasted, sometimes stuffed with nuts and raisins. Meat was also combined with vegetables - onions, carrots, turnips, spinach, aubergines and herbs such as parsley and dill, and cooked in oil, butter or ghee - to make rich stews. One of the specialities of Iranian cuisine was *faisenjan*, a dish of chicken, duck or sturgeon steaks simmered in a subtly flavoured sauce of pomegranate juice and walnuts. Vegetables were also cooked as main dishes, including delicious variations of aubergines, courgettes and onions stuffed with mixtures of rice, minced meat, herbs and dried fruits. Other

Painted papier mâché playing cards. Iran, 19th century.

wrapped and stuffed foods were the Turkish *börek*, where parcels of cheese, meat, spinach, or pumpkin, were folded inside sheets of fine papery pastry in triangular, coiled and rectangular shapes, and the Iranian *kuku*, a thick omelette with rich fillings of green herbs, potatoes and aubergines.

Rice was served both as a base for all these foods and cooked into splendid dishes in their own right. Turkish *pilaus* were flavoured with carrots, currants, aubergines and chicken livers. Iranian cuisine developed the cooking of rice into a great culinary art, in which apricots, sour cherries and orange peel, spinach and green beans, chicken, and lamb were assembled into glistening coloured mounds, garnished with saffron and pistachio nuts. A tempting array of side-dishes accompanied these meals, including seasonal salads, sharp cucumbers served in yoghurt and home-made pickles. Drinks were plain water, diluted yoghurt, or refreshing sherbets of lemon, orange and pomegranate juices, rose and cherry syrups. The meal traditionally finished with a selection of seasonal fruits, such as melons, oranges, cherries, peaches, apricots, grapes, or a compote of dried fruit in winter. Coffee was normally only prepared at intervals during the day and offered with sweets to guests. Both were served after dinner as a European-style meal service was introduced.

After supper, family evenings were spent together in conversation in the main reception room of the *haremlik*, where snacks of sweets and dried fruits were served. The men could depart to the *selamlık* to talk among themselves. Depending on education and aptitude there was a choice of activity. Turkish and Iranian women and girls, as well as working on fine pieces of embroidery, often specialized in gourmet cooking, preparing confectionery and adventurous main dishes. Lady Sheil records that:

Painted papier mâché pen box and tray. Kashmir, 19th century

One of the princesses, whose husband was of similar rank, and was on intimate terms of acquaintance with my husband, used frequently to send me savoury dishes at our dinner hour. An intimation always accompanied the viands, of their being the preparation of the 'Shazadeh Khanum', the lady princess, herself. Sometimes a very young lamb, roasted whole, decked with flowers, with a rich stuffing of chestnuts or pistachios, would appear as our *pièce de resistance*.

In a well-educated household both sexes would spend time in reading, writing and calligraphy. From the sixteenth century the presence and names of women appear in classical and experimental poetry, and as copiers of religious texts exquisitely written in various scripts. The day's activities finished with the night prayer just before the family retired to bed.

Detail of a battle scene from a manuscript of the poet Nizami's epic Khusrau and Shirin. *Iran, Tabriz, attributed to Mir Sayyid 'Ali, c1540*

5
SOCIAL AND PUBLIC LIFE

> On a sofa, raised three steps, and covered with fine Persian carpets, sat the *Kiyaya's* lady, leaning on two cushions of white satin, embroidered; at her feet sat two young girls, the eldest about twelve years old, lovely as angels, dressed perfectly rich, and almost covered with jewels... She stood up to receive me, saluting me after their fashion, putting her hand upon her heart with a sweetness full of majesty ... She ordered cushions to be given to me, and took care to place me in the corner, which is the place of honour.
>
> She told me the two maids were her daughters, though she appeared too young to be their mother. Her fair maids ranged below the sofa, to the number of twenty... they served me coffee upon their knees in the finest Japan china, with soucoupes of silver gilt...

Lady Mary Wortley Montagu's account of her visit to the wife of the steward of Sultan Ahmet III in 1717 describes hospitality on the grand scale. The rituals of receiving and returning visits enabled members of a family, especially the women, to move out of their own private space. Most Ottoman women of high social position had a weekly at-home day in the *haremlik* when they entertained a wide circle of friends. These occasions were opportunities to exhibit textiles in a splendid dress display, and to exchange gifts of embroidery.

After the formal courtesies of welcome had been given, guests were offered coffee, tea, preserves, flaky pastries laden with ground almonds, pistachios or walnuts and soaked in honey, at steady intervals throughout the visit. The preparation of coffee was accompanied by much ritual in small kitchens attached to both *haremlik* and *selamlık* which were equipped with pans for roasting and mills for grinding coffee beans to a fine powder. The coffee was brewed thick and strong in a long-handled spouted copper pot and served in small cups. Flavours varied according to the quality of the beans and the addition of sugar and aromatics.

Depending on the formality of the visit, guests brought their small children with them. They would join their hostess to embroider and to exchange news and gossip. Women pedlars, who knew all a neighbourhood's reception days, would arrive with bundles of fabrics and ready-made articles, sure of good business. Before the introduction of reasonably efficient wheeled transport in the seventeenth century, prior to the use of coach and landau, guests would frequently stay overnight.

Accommodation of numerous visitors was never a problem in either *haremlik* or *selamlık*, as mattresses and quilts were taken out of wall cupboards and spread on the floor. A parallel social life went on in the *selamlık*, but men also had the chance of visiting

Istanbul, ladies drinking coffee. Count Amadeo Preziosi, 1853

*Istanbul, coffee
house. Count Amadeo
Preziosi, 1853*

*Ceramic coffee cups.
Turkey, Kutahya,
18th century*

coffee and teahouses which were established in all Middle Eastern cities, where they were entertained by musicians, dancers and storytellers.

While both sexes pursued effectively separate lives there were occasions other than visits for women to leave the cloister of the *harem* apartments and enter a more public sphere. One of the most popular, because it could take place throughout the year and was an opportunity to extend a woman's social circle, was the weekly visit to the *hammam*, the public bath. Women of the palaces were confined to private *hammams* built within their apartments. However, women of households wealthy enough to have their own *hammam*, often chose to visit the public baths for company and diversion. All Middle Eastern cities were well supplied with public baths, ranging from the monumental structures endowed as conspicuous acts of charity, such as the splendid domed *hammam* commissioned by Hürrem, wife of Süleyman the Magnificent, built near the Topkapi Saray in the sixteenth century, to the more modest building of each residential quarter.

Women treated a visit to the bath as a full day's excursion. They took everything that they required: rugs and cushions, embroidered towels and napkins, bowls and soap, bath clogs, supplies of oils and perfumes, picnic lunch and their embroidery. While every room in every household had ewers and basins of water for morning and evening ablutions, the rituals of cleansing before prayer, and washing hands before and after meals, the *hammam* was equipped for serious cleansing and pampering. Each *hammam* consisted of a series of rooms in ascending degrees of heat which converged on a large hall furnished with a heated marble platform surrounded by basins and fountains of water. Here the bathers were scrubbed, depilated, massaged, showered and shampooed. Hair

Iran, Semnan. Entrance to the town's hammam, *early 20th century*

Glazed ceramic pumices. Iran, 17th and 19th centuries

was conditioned and dyed, and nails, hands and feet were hennaed. There were breaks for refreshments of tea, coffee and food, gossip and sewing, between all these energetic processes. Men could also participate in the comforts of the *hammam*, and in fact would visit them frequently for shorter visits than those of the women. Their rituals were less relaxing, involving brisk scrubbing and a tortuous form of massage which folded and cracked the limbs to make the joints supple.

Less arduous excursions enjoyed by both men and women, were made possible by the introduction of efficient transport, relative liberalization of social conventions, and the changes in facilities created by the building programmes of the 1860s-70s. Upper-class and middle-class women who traditionally inspected goods for sale in their homes, ventured out discreetly cloaked and veiled on shopping expeditions, both to the bazaars and the new European-style shops. In Istanbul, a popular outing was to the Pera quarter where the Grand Rue de Pera was lined with smart shops and chic dress boutiques. Excursions to local beauty spots were another diversion. Upper-class women in Istanbul would travel about in an *araba*, a small covered wagon hung with fringed textiles and furnished with quilts and cushions, to view public events such as reviews of the Sultan's troops, illuminations of the great palaces and homes of the Bosphorus, and to enjoy picnics in the agreeable suburbs of the Golden Horn. Informal family picnics were one of the pleasures of social life in Iran, as enjoyed by Dr C J Wills in Isfahan in the late nineteenth century.

> An invitation to [a picnic] is generally given without any preparation, as during the paying of a call; it is accepted, and forthwith an immediate start is made. A few carpets and pillows are rolled up and placed on a mule, with the samovar or Russian urn in its leather case, and the tea Equipage in its travelling box. The cook, on his pony, takes his whole *batterie de cuisine* and hurries to the garden indicated by his master, probably buying a lamp and a couple of fowls, as he passes through the bazaar. The entertainer, his wife and children too, if we are very intimate, the former on his horse, the latter astride on white donkeys, proceed at a leisurely pace in the direction of the garden; while the servants, all smiles, for they enjoy the outing as much as the family, accompany them on foot or horseback, carrying waterpipes, umbrellas and odds and ends. On reaching the garden, fruit is eaten; then the whole party roam unrestricted among the shady paths while tea is prepared. This is partaken of, and then a musician, or a singer, or perhaps a story-teller, makes his appearance and diverts us all. Or some servant, who has a good voice, sings or plays on the flute to us.

Excursions could satisfy the needs for both social diversion and religious piety by taking the form of a visit to a local shrine. In Istanbul pilgrims had a wide choice, from the stately shrine of Eyüp Ensari, standard bearer of the Prophet Muhammad, at the top of the Golden Horn to more homely places such as the grave of Telli Baba up at Rumeli Kavağı, whose aid was frequently invoked by anxious mothers and daughters seeking eligible

Istanbul, women and children in a bathhouse. Camille Rogier, 1840-43

suitors. Within distance of the south of Tehran was the glittering sanctuary of Shah Abdul Azim at Rayy, while the city itself was honeycombed with small local shrines.

A consistent shape and rhythm to the daily routine was given by the interwoven patterns of family celebrations and the calendar of Muslim religious festivals, which all gave occasion for generous hospitality and display in wealthy establishments. Family celebrations often involved a subtle interplay between the private and public world. They were unique activities performed in the context of the rituals for giving and receiving hospitality, with the most important ceremonies marking the traditional rites of passage: birth, circumcision, marriage and death.

Birth rites were exclusively the province of women in households from the royal palaces down to the homes of the poor. Children were much cherished in Middle Eastern society, and although the preference was for boys, the entry of any child into the world was greeted with much rejoicing. In élite Ottoman society, immediately after the birth the baby was washed and then wrapped in swaddling bands, followed by layers of printed and embroidered cloths, and taken to its mother. She had been dressed in her richest clothes and laid on a couch adorned with all the household's finest textiles. Julia Pardoe's 1837 account of her visit to the wife of a judge in Bursa conveys the impact of such a scene.

> Directly opposite to the door stood the bed of the Hanoum; the curtains had been withdrawn, and a temporary canopy formed of cachemire shawls arranged in festoons and linked together with bathing scarves of gold and silver tissue: and, as the lady was possessed of fifty, which could not all be arranged with proper effect in so limited a space, a silk cord had been stretched along the ceiling to the opposite extremity of the apartment, over which the costly drapery was continued. Fastened to the shawls were head-dresses of coloured gauze, flowered or striped with gold and silver, whence depended oranges, lemons and candied fruits. Two coverlets of wadded pink satin were folded at the bed's foot; and a sheet of striped crape hung to the floor, where it terminated in a deep fringe of gold.
>
> The infant lay upon a cushion of white satin richly embroidered with coloured silks, and trimmed like the sheet; and was itself a mass of gold brocade and diamonds.

From the third to seventh day the mother received guests who brought gifts of jewellery, ornaments, fabrics and sweets all wrapped in embroidered cloths. On the seventh day the child was transferred to a cradle and the elaborate bed was dismantled. The last ceremony took place on the fortieth day when the mother and baby went to the *hammam* for a leisurely party. Here, pampered by friends and attendants, they were washed and groomed. This cycle of events accompanied the birth of children to the Sultan with some significant variations. The mother lay on a magnificent couch, draped in red satin adorned with rubies, emeralds and pearls, colours and gems associated with the Ottoman dynasty. Royal family ceremonies were not entirely private as the family were obliged to entertain the public with feasts and processions. The royal child received three cradles,

Celebrations at the birth of a child. India, Deccan, late 17th century

Horse groomed and adorned for a procession. India, Kishengarh, c1820

one prepared by the Imperial Treasury, and two given by the Sultan's mother and the Grand Vizir. These two were paraded together with quilts and covers and gifts of jewellery along a route from the area of the bazaar, down past the mosque of Aya Sofya and around to the gate of the Topkapi Saray where they were escorted to the *haremlik*.

Circumcision of all Muslim boys marked their entry into the men's world. Sometimes babies were circumcised on the fortieth day after their birth, at the mother's bath ceremony. Generally, however, the occasion was very important, and most boys were circumcised at about the age of seven. To prepare them for the operation they were dressed in special clothes, and taken around their neighbourhood in procession. Edward Lane in Cairo notes:

> A horse, handsomely caparisoned, is also borrowed to convey him; and in his hand is placed a folded embroidered handkerchief, which he constantly holds before his mouth in his right hand, to hide part of his face, and thus protect himself from the evil eye. He is preceded by a servant of the barber, who is the operator, and by three or more musicians, whose instruments are commonly a hautboy and drums.

Linen hanging embroidered with a design of stylized carnations. Turkey, 17th century

After the circumcision the boy was laid on a couch hung with splendid textiles where he received visitors bringing gifts, in the same manner as his mother had done at his birth. While this ceremony was one of great pride to a boy's family, the circumcision of a Sultan's son was an occasion for public rejoicing when processions of courtiers and tradesmen enlivened the streets of Istanbul. People decorated the streets with their household textiles, draping them over house fronts as banners, and lining the processional route with them.

Marriage was essentially a contractual arrangement between the two families, often requiring long negotiation in which the bride and groom had little part. They certainly did not see each other until the last day of the wedding festivities. While boys took marriage for granted, and Islam does not encourage celibacy, the search for an eligible husband was a subject of much thought and effort for women and their daughters. Girls were introduced to the importance of marriage early, as they spent most of their leisure time sewing and embroidering household linens and clothing for their trousseaux and knew that they were expected to be married between the ages of twelve and fourteen years. Mothers at all levels of society relentlessly canvassed relatives and friends through their networks of hospitality and the *hammam* for possible candidates. Attractive daughters were paraded in the *harems* to female negotiators who would then report to the boy's family.

Once two families were in agreement, preparations were made for the formal engagement. This required discussion of the bride's trousseau and the *mehr*, the contribution from the bridegroom which was an obligation in Muslim marriage. The bridegroom agreed a sum of money in two parts, one to contribute towards the cost of the wedding and the new home and the other to be endowed on the bride. This was her inalienable right, to be administered as she chose and to be used as alimony in case of divorce. The engagement concluded with an exchange of gifts between groom and bride and the signing of the contract. The groom's gifts included fabric for the wedding dress, and a set of jewellery casket, mirror, bowl and clogs for the bath.

The wedding usually followed the engagement promptly, although it could be postponed for good reasons, such as the extreme youth of the bridal couple. Wedding festivities consisted of a week of parties and celebrations in both *selamlık* and *haremlik* accompanied by spectacular processions in the wealthiest families. This time-honoured ritual was followed throughout the Middle East, but was possibly most lavishly celebrated by the Ottoman Sultan's family.

The programme began on a Monday with the procession of the bride's trousseau through the streets to the groom's home. Here years of hard work of sewing and embroidery were rewarded as covers, pillows, curtains, sets of bedding and clothes were carried on open trays. The splendour of such textile display is seen in Julia Pardoe's

Detail from a sampler of needle-lace (oya) borders. Turkey, 19th century

description of the trousseau procession of Mihrimah, daughter of Sultan Mahmut II in the 1830s.

> But the most gorgeous display was yet to come; embroidered handkerchiefs whose gold and silver threads were mingled with silks of many hues, and whose texture was almost as impalpable as the gossamer-jackets of velvet worked on the sleeves and hearts with precious stones - trousers sprinkled with stars of gold and silver - anteries of white silk, wreathed with coloured jewels - robes of satin powdered with seed-pearls - slippers as diminutive as that of Cinderella, fringed with floss silk and powdered with rubies; and finally, sixteen bearers, balancing upon their head cages of silver wire, resting on cushions of crimson velvet, whereupon were displayed the bridal diamonds. The sunshine was flashing on them as they passed us, and at times it was impossible to look upon them.

Embroidered velvet wedding dress. Turkey, late 19th century

Once the trousseau had arrived, the bride's relatives and friends hung, draped and twisted the textiles around her rooms. The remaining days were mainly devoted to adorning and dressing the bride.

On Tuesday she went to the bath to be soaped, massaged and perfumed, on Wednesday she received and entertained her bridegroom's female relatives and friends. The wedding preparations came to a climax on Wednesday evening and Thursday morning when the bride was finally adorned and dressed. The 'henna night' which took place on Wednesday was an old Middle Eastern custom which predated Islam, and symbolized the bride's farewell to her girlhood. It was a lively party attended by dancers and musicians if the family was wealthy. The bride's mother-in-law painted the girl's hands and feet with henna paste. The bridegroom, his friends and relatives meanwhile

Egyptian dancing girls at Rosetta. Prisse d'Avennes, 1848

Detail from a silk tomb cover. Turkey, 17th century

were enjoying a rowdy party. On Thursday morning, after the henna had dried and was brushed off to reveal bright patterns in orange-red, the bride was dressed in the wedding garments sent as a present from the groom.

The main dress in the case of a Turkish bride was traditionally made of deep crimson or purple velvet heavily embroidered in gold or silver with bold flower motifs, although later silks in light colours such as oyster, shell pink and mauve were introduced. Gold and silver completed the outfit, plaited as fine threads in her hair and applied as sequins and glittering powder to her whitened and rouged face. Shrouded in a red veil, the bride was escorted by the groom's family to the decorated rooms of her new home, where she was displayed to the female guests. The evening passed in celebrations in both *selamlık* and *haremlik*. Friday marked the end of the wedding ceremony, where the bride and groom appeared together before the family and a lavish feast was served consisting of a huge dish of wedding rice coloured yellow with saffron, rich meat stews and an abundance of sweets and fruit.

Funerals, the last rite of passage, were relatively simple and took place by sunset of the day of death. As the coffin was taken in procession from the home to the mosque for prayers and then to the grave, a man's turban or a woman's headscarf and hair ornaments were laid upon it. In the great imperial tomb chambers of the Ottoman imperial family, in Istanbul and Bursa, elaborately carved and tiled structures were erected over the graves and draped with cloths woven or embroidered with religious inscriptions, and sometimes with garments of the deceased.

The Muslim year was based on a lunar calendar of twelve months which revolved independently of the seasons, but was punctuated by

Shah Sultan Hussein (1694-1722) distributing New Year gifts. Iran, Isfahan, by Muhammad 'Ali, dated 1721

a succession of religious ceremonies. Some of these were occasions for joyful celebration and feasts, others were days of mourning, and yet others passed with little attention.

New Year's Day, being simply the first day of the first month, was not generally marked with more than an exchange of greetings and good wishes. This low-key observance was because New Year's Day was immediately followed by ten days of prayer and lamentation for the death in battle of the Imam Hussein, grandson of the Prophet Muhammad, which culminated in the great processions of mourners on the tenth day, Ashura. These events were commemorated with special fervour by the Shi'a Muslims of Iran where they were accompanied by passion plays dramatizing the life of the martyr Hussein. A special food was prepared for this occasion, a dish in locally varying combinations of rice, wheat grains, pulses, dried fruits, nuts, honey and sugar boiled and simmered into a rich pudding.

Iranians also celebrated an additional New Year, the ancient spring festival of *Nou Ruz* meaning 'New Day'. This joyful occasion began on 21 March, independently of

Photograph of the court official Muhammad Hussein Mirza taken in the late 19th century

Length of wool fabric woven with repeated floral motifs. Iran, Kerman, late 19th century

the Muslim calendar. It was celebrated with lavish gifts of new clothes to the social élite. In 1850 Nasiruddin Shah 'bestows on all his courtiers some mark of his bounty; Cashmere shawls to those of high rank; descending thence in a sliding-scale to cloth coats and spangled muslin'. Families joined in a meal which always included herbs and fruit. Two weeks holiday followed, which provided an opportunity to visit relatives and enjoy picnics and excursions.

The next event of the Muslim year was also a joyful occasion. The birthday of the Prophet Muhammad on the 27th day of the third month was celebrated with prayers in all the mosques, readings of narrative poems of the Prophet's life, and processions and performances by dancers and jugglers. Rich families in Turkey decorated their homes and gardens with lamps and lanterns and distributed gifts of sweets in embroidered silk and satin bags. The year continued with a succession of holy nights, such as the anniversary of the Prophet's miraculous journey to heaven, and the sombre Night of Destiny, when mankind's fate was cast and all sins were absolved.

The most important month was the ninth month of Ramazan, when all Muslims were obliged to fast from sunrise to sunset although the month was also an opportunity for relaxation and enjoyment. During the evenings, the cities were alive with activity and the mosques were illuminated and remained open all night. People thronged the streets, shopping and visiting. The *iftar* meal taken after sunset was an occasion for wealthy families to enhance their social prestige through generous hospitality. This custom continued into the early twentieth century as Emine Foat Tugay recorded of her family:

An Imam and a muezzin were engaged for the whole month at our house, and the latter would chant the call to evening prayer from

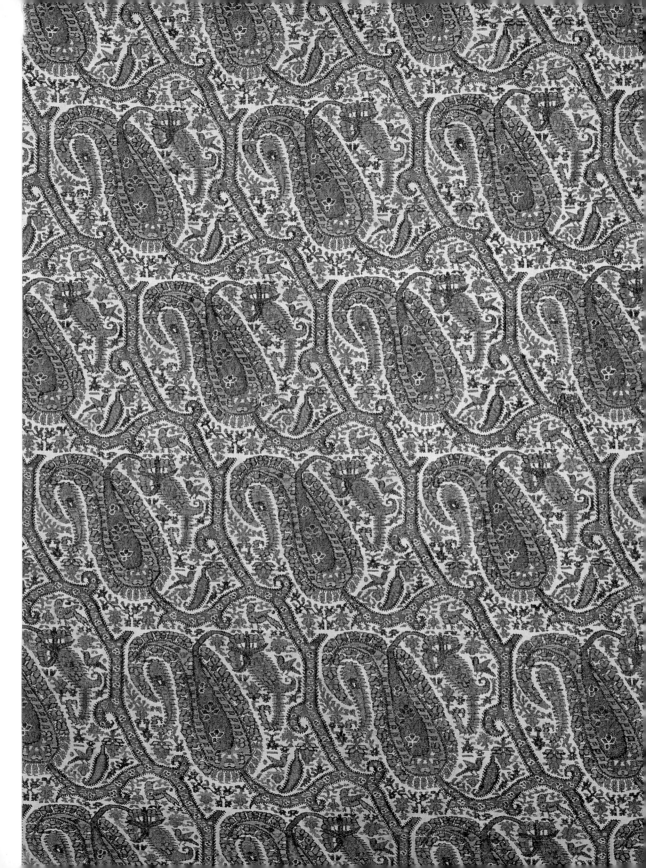

Index